Phr

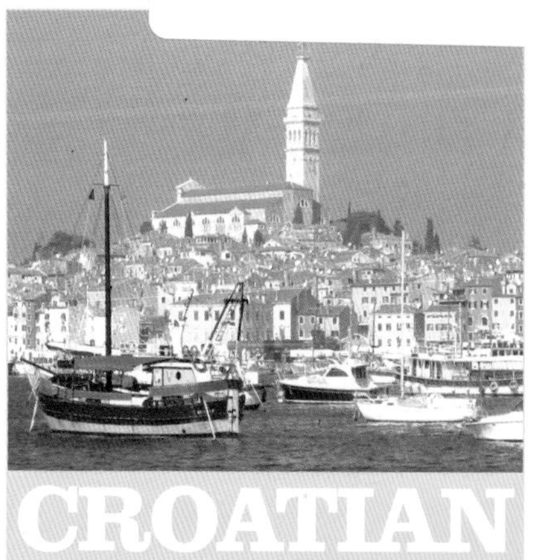

CROATIAN

With menu decoder, survival guide and two-way dictionary

www.thomascookpublishing.com

Survival guide....................49

Emergencies....................59

Dictionary....................63

Quick reference....................95

How to use this guide

The ten chapters in this guide are colour-coded to help you find what you're looking for. These colours are used on the tabs of the pages and in the contents on the opposite page and above.

For quick reference, you'll find some basic expressions on the inside front cover and essential emergency phrases on the inside back cover. There is also a handy reference section for numbers, measurements and clothes sizes at the back of the guide.

Front cover photography © JadroFoto/Alamy Images
Cover design/artwork by Sharon Edwards
Photo credits: Hotel Jadran (p13), Make life sweeter! – http://linda.kovacevic.nl (p18), Agroturizam Ograde (p20), Phillip Collier (p25), Nina Jecić, Licitar studio (p35), Residence Parentino (p43), Adriatica.net (p44) and Kenneth De Buck (p46)

Produced by The Content Works Ltd
www.thecontentworks.com
Design concept: Mike Wade
Layout: Tika Stefano & Pat Hinsley
Text: Gorana Nad-Conlan
Editing: Sanja Adamović & Amanda Castleman
Proofing: Wendy Janes
Project editor: Begoña Juarros
Management: Lisa Plumridge & Rik Mulder

Published by Thomas Cook Publishing
A division of Thomas Cook Tour Operations Limited
Company Registration No 1450464 England
PO Box 227, Unit 18, Coningsby Road
Peterborough PE3 8SB, United Kingdom
email: books@thomascook.com
www.thomascookpublishing.com
+44 (0)1733 416477

ISBN-13: 978-1-84157-669-5

Project Editor: Kelly Pipes
Production/DTP: Steven Collins

Printed and bound in Italy by Printer Trento

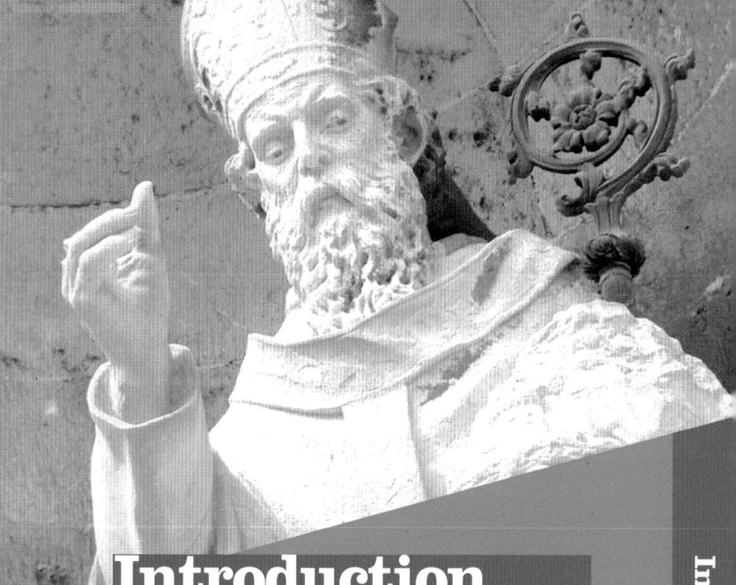

Introduction

Croatian – **hrvatski jezik** – is the official language of the Republic of Croatia, and one of three in Bosnia and Herzegovina. Charlemagne's army left traces of Latin in this tongue, but it was also influenced by other invaders: the Habsburgs, Ottomans and Venetians. Part of the western group of South Slavic languages, it shares some traits with Czech, Russian and Polish, as well as its close siblings Macedonian, Serbian and Slovenian. In fact, Croatian can be understood across former Yugoslavia, so don't ditch this phrasebook at the border!

The basics

Much like its speakers, the Croatian language has had a turbulent and varied past. Slavic tribes brought it one thousand miles from the Carpathian marshlands to modern-day Slavonia and Dalmatia, where the written form dates back to the 9th century.

These Croats used the Glagolitic alphabet, which resembled cursive Greek. Their descendants proudly point to a 1248 papal dispensation allowing their nation, alone in Europe, to hold mass in this tongue. Eventually the Latin alphabet prevailed – and that script is still used today. However, some of its 30 letters are adorned with distinctive diacritics (the acute accent; the **háček** – like a tiny 'v') and certain familiar characters are absent: q, x and y.

In contrast with English, Croatian looks as it reads: each letter represents a distinctive sound and every sound is represented by a single letter. Complicated at first, once you learn the pronunciation rules, they never change. Beginners can usually read Croatian rather quickly.

The Croatian language has three dialects: **štokavski**, **čakavski** and **kajkavski** . A simple way to distinguish between them is the pronoun "what": **što**, **ča** and **kaj** respectively. **Štokavski** became the official dialect, but **kajkavski** is very much alive in Zagreb and its surroundings, both in vernacular and some very fine literature. And **čakavski** is still spoken along the coast and the islands.

In times past, Croatian lands have often played unwilling host to other nations and empires, be it Ottomans, Austro-Hungarians or Italians.

Monument to language

The single most important monument to Croatian literacy is a stone tablet from the late 11th century. You can see it in the small church of Sv Lucija on the island of Krk, written in the Glagolitic script.

Through much of its modern history, Croatia was part of Yugoslavia, first as a kingdom and then as a socialist federal republic. This period encouraged unification of Croatian and Serbian – separate but mutually intelligible languages – into one, Serbo-Croatian tongue.

Today, regional dialects and slang contain many everyday words that sprang from these influences; the coast and Istria, in particular, have their own peculiar take on Italian. The German-influenced people of Zagreb and the interior regions still present each other with a **gešenk** ("das Geschenk" – gift), give **tringlt** to waiters ("das Trinkgeld" – a tip) and have **fruštuk** in the morning ("das Frühstück" – breakfast). Turkish words are peppered throughout the land. And **Palačinke** – those lovely thin pancakes filled with jam, chopped walnuts or chocolate – carry a name of Hungarian origin. These words are all part of a rich vibrant tapestry of living Croatian.

Grammar

Here's the simplest way to express an idea happening now. Just take the infinitive – the "to do" form listed in the dictionary – and lop off last three letters:

zn-ati	**rad-iti**	**pis-ati**
to know	to work	to write

Now add the appropriate ending:

ja I	**zn-am** know	**rad-im** work	**piš-em** write
ti you	**zn-aš** know	**rad-iš** work	**piš-eš** write
on, ona, ono he/she/it	**zn-a** knows	**rad-i** works	**piš-e** writes
mi we	**zn-amo** know	**rad-imo** work	**piš-emo** write
vi you (plural)	**zn-ate** know	**rad-ite** work	**piš-ete** write
oni, one they	**zn-aju** know	**rad-e** work	**piš-u** write

Other verbs that you can conjugate using these patterns are in the dictionary section. To swim (**plivati**), to enjoy (**uživati**), to ask (**pitati**), to have (**imati**) and to sleep (**spavati**) all follow the pattern for **znati**. To smoke (**pušiti**), to drive (**voziti**) and to kiss (**ljubiti**) follow the pattern for **raditi**. To breathe (**disati**) and to smell sweet (**mirisati**) follow the pattern for **pisati**.

Unfortunately, many verbs – including essentials like "to be", "to love", "to eat", and "to help" – are irregular and require brute memorization. And if all the study and č, ć, dž, đ, š and ž characters become overwhelming, just point, smile and soldier onward. Any effort to speak Croatian will earn you friends for life.

Basic conversation

Hello	**Zdravo**	*zdravo*
Goodbye	**Doviđenja**	*doveejeniya*
Yes	**Da**	*da*
No	**Ne**	*ne*
Please	**Molim**	*moleem*
Thank you	**Hvala**	*hvala*
You're welcome	**Molim**	*moleem*
Sorry	**Žalim**	*zhaleem*
Excuse me (apology, to get attention, to pass)	**Oprostite**	*oprosteete*
Do you speak English?	**Govorite li engleski?**	*govoreete lee engleskee?*
I don't speak Croatian	**Ne govorim hrvatski**	*ne govoreem her-vatskee*
I speak a little Croatian	**Malo govorim hrvatski**	*malo govoreem her-vatskee*
What?	**Što?**	*shto?*
I understand	**Razumijem**	*razoomeeyem*
I don't understand	**Ne razumijem**	*ne razoomeeyem*
Do you understand?	**Razumijete li?**	*razoomeeyete lee?*
I don't know	**Ne znam**	*ne znam*
I can't	**Ne mogu**	*ne mogoo*
Can you... please?	**Možete li… molim Vas?**	*mozhete lee... moleem vas?*
- speak more slowly	**- govoriti malo polaganije**	*- govoreetee malo polaganeeye*
- repeat that	**- ponoviti**	*- ponoveetee*

Greetings

Traditionally, Croatian still makes the distinction between addressing a mate or your partner's great aunt. First names are for friends; venerables have earned their titles, surnames and the plural form. Although the starchy traditions are relaxing, do not be surprised to be called "Mr, Mrs or Miss". Return the favour to avoid social faux pas: your elders and betters will request further intimacy, if it's welcome. Shake hands on first meeting and remember to keep eye contact, especially when making a toast.

Meeting someone

Hello	**Zdravo**	*zdravo*
Hi	**Bok**	*bok*
Good morning	**Dobro jutro**	*dobro yootro*
Good afternoon	**Dobar dan**	*dobar dan*
Good evening	**Dobra večer**	*dobra vecher*
Cheers!	**Živjeli!**	*zheeviyelee!*
Sir/Mr	**Gospodin**	*gospodeen*
Madam/Mrs	**Gospođa**	*gospoja*
Miss	**Gospođica**	*gospojeetsa*
How are you?	**Kako ste?**	*kako ste?*
Fine, thank you	**Dobro, hvala**	*dobro, hvala*
And you?	**A Vi?**	*a vee?*
Very well	**Vrlo dobro**	*verlo dobro*
Not very well	**Ne baš dobro**	*ne bash dobro*

Say cheers!

Toasting happens with remarkable frequency in Croatia. Raise a glass of Karlovac beer, a **bevanda** (red wine and water), **rakija** (fruit schnapps) or **travarica** (fruit schnapps with herbs) and look your drinking partners in the eye as you clink glasses. **Zivjeli!**

Small talk

My name is...	**Moje je ime...**	*moyea ye eeme...*
What's your name?	**Kako Vam je ime?**	*kako vam ye eeme?*
I'm pleased to meet you	**Drago mi je**	*drago mee ye*
Where are you from?	**Otkuda ste?**	*otkooda ste?*
I am from Britain	**Ja sam iz Britanije**	*ya sam iz breetaniye*

Do you live here?	**Živite li ovdje?**	*zheeveete lee ovdiyea?*
This is a...	**Ovo je...**	*ovo ye...*
- great country	**- sjajna zemlja**	*- siyayna zemliya*
- great city/town	**- sjajan grad**	*- siyayan grad*
I am staying at...	**Ja boravim u...**	*ya boraveem oo...*
I'm just here for the day	**Ovdje sam samo jedan dan**	*ovdiyea sam samo yedan dan*
I'm in... for...	**U... ostajem...**	*oo... ostayem...*
- a weekend	**- za vikend**	*- za veekend*
- a week	**- tjedan dana**	*- tiyedan dana*
How old are you?	**Koliko Vam je godina?**	*koleeko vam ye godeena?*
I'm... years old	**Ja imam... godina**	*ya eemam... godeena*

Family

This is my...	**Ovo je...**	*ovo ye...*
- husband	**- moj suprug**	*- moy sooproog*
- wife	**- moja supruga**	*- moya sooprooga*
- partner	**- moj partner/moja partnerica**	*- moy partner/moya partnereetsa*
- boyfriend/ girlfriend	**- moj dečko/moja djevojka**	*- moy dechko/moya diyevoyka*
I have a...	**Imam...**	*eemam...*
- son	**- sina**	*- seena*
- daughter	**- kćer**	*- kcher*
- grandson	**- unuka**	*- oonooka*
- granddaughter	**- unuku**	*- oonookoo*
Do you have...	**Imate li...**	*eemate lee...*
- children?	**- djece?**	*- diyetse?*
- grandchildren?	**- unuka?**	*- oonooka?*
I don't have children	**Ja nemam djece**	*ya nemam diyetse*
Are you married?	**Jeste li u braku?**	*yeste lee oo braku?*
I'm...	**Ja sam...**	*ya sam...*
- single	**- neoženjen** *m*	*- neozheniyen*
	- neudata *f*	*- neoodata*
- married	**- oženjen** *m*	*- ozheniyen*
	- udata *f*	*- oodata*

You say hello and I say goodbye

In informal Croatian, you can say **bok** for either. Sometimes pronounced "bog", it originates as a word for God, the phrase having probably started as "go with God". On the coast, **adio** is an easy-to-remember farewell.

- divorced	**- razveden** *m*	*- razveden*
	- razvedena *f*	*- razvedena*
- widowed	**- udovac** *m*	*- oodovats*
	- udovica *f*	*- oodoveetsa*

Saying goodbye

Goodbye	**Doviđenja**	*doveejeniya*
Good night	**Laku noć**	*lakoo noch*
Sleep well	**Ugodan san**	*oogodan san*
See you later	**Vidimo se**	*veedeemo se*
Have a good trip	**Sretan put**	*sretan poot*
It was nice meeting you	**Bilo mi je drago**	*beelo mee ye drago*
All the best	**Sve najbolje**	*sve naiybolyea*
Have fun	**Uživajte**	*oozheevayte*
Good luck	**Sretno**	*sretno*
Keep in touch	**Ostanimo u kontaktu**	*ostanimo oo kontaktoo*
My address is...	**Moja adresa je...**	*moya adresa ye...*
What's your...	**Koja je Vaša...**	*koya ye vasha...*
- address/email?	**- adresa/email adresa?**	*- adresa/eemail adresa?*
What's your telephone number?	**Koji je vaš broj telefona?**	*koyee ye vash broy telefona?*

Eating out

Croatia sits at the crossroads of Continental, Mediterranean and Eastern traditions. Together with abundant nature, this creates a small but perfectly formed melting pot of seriously good food. Restaurant choice and menu variety may not be huge, but the ingredients are superbly fresh, locally sourced, seasonal and – more often than not – organic. Food here has an important, proud place in people's lives. Croats love to share their passions and, whether it happens at the family table or in a restaurant, the result is almost always a memorable meal.

Introduction

Here, restaurants are considered life's great pleasure, while cafés with outside tables are an absolute necessity. These are places in which to sip coffee or beer and watch the world go by, rather then eat, so fill up at pizzerias, taverns or seafood restaurants. All serve alcohol, except patisseries.

I'd like...	**Molio/Molila** *m/f* **bih...**	*moleeo/moleela beeh...*
- a table for two	**- stol za dvoje**	*- stol za dvoye*
- a sandwich	**- sendvič**	*- sendveech*
- a coffee	**- kavu**	*- kavoo*
- a tea (with milk)	**- čaj (s mlijekom)**	*- chaiy (s mleeyekom)*
Do you have a menu in English?	**Imate li jelovnik na engleskom?**	*eemate lee yelovneek na engleskom?*
The bill, please	**Račun molim**	*rachoon moleem*

You may hear...

Pušačko ili nepušačko mjesto?	*pooshachko eelee nepooshachko miyesto?*	Smoking or non-smoking?
Što ćete naručiti?	*shto chete naroocheetee?*	What are you going to have?

The cuisines of Croatia

National specialities

Although distinctly regional, much of Croatian cuisine centres around meat, often slow-simmered in its own juices. Traditionally, lamb or veal shanks are cooked in the cinders of an open fire, a method dating back 3,000 years. Today, a covered cast-iron pot – **peka** – is the norm.

Signature dishes

(see the Menu decoder for more dishes)

Škampi na buzaru	*shkampee na boozaroo*	Scampi, garlic, parsley and wine
Janjetina s ražnja	*yanyeteena s razhnya*	Spit-roast lamb

Crni rižoto	*tsernee reezhoto*	"Black risotto" with cuttlefish ink
Žablji krakovi	*zhablyee krakovee*	Fried frogs' legs

Waiting to be seated?
Don't linger in restaurant doorways. You're wasting valuable time, as it is not customary for waiters to greet guests. Be bolshy and sit down.

Zagreb

Zagreb offers excellent Continental choice, but also has some very good seafood restaurants. On the slopes of Sljeme you'll find several excellent eateries with authentic food and atmosphere. Or climb further and join hikers for a bean stew and mulled wine. Zagreb boasts some of the country's best pizza places.

Signature dishes

(see the Menu decoder for more dishes)

Zagrebački odrezak	*zagrebachkee odrezak*	Breaded veal/pork stuffed with ham, cheese
Fileki	*feelekee*	Tripe
Grah	*grah*	Bean stew with cured meats
Paprenjaci	*paprenyatsee*	Pepper and honey biscuits
Gratinirani štrukli	*grateeneeranee shtrooklee*	Baked pastries with curd cheese

Zagorje

This region's rustic cooking has mesmerised Croats for centuries. They've sung the praises of versatile Zagorje puddings in traditional and rock tunes, while poultry with **mlinci** (local pasta) takes pride of place at the Christmas table. For a day trip, go to Veliki tabor and explore the local inn menus.

Signature dishes
(see the Menu decoder for more dishes)

Štrukli	*shtrooklee*	Pastries with curd cheese
Zaseka	*zaseka*	Bacon pâté
Pura s mlincima	*poora s mleentseema*	Turkey with local pasta
Zagorska plata	*zagorska plata*	Platter of local meats, cheeses
Zlevanka or **bazlamača**	*zlevanka bazlamacha*	Traditional polenta cake

Slavonia

Slavonia is a region of fertile lands, rich cuisine, ornate costumes and industrious people. But no matter how hard Slavonians work, they still struggle to meet the demand for authentic **kulen** sausage, one of Croatia's best. Luckily, there are always hams, cheeses, game and abundant freshwater fish to fall back on...

Signature dishes
(see the Menu decoder for more dishes)

Kulen	*koolen*	Spicy red paprika sausage
Slavonski čobanac	*slavonskee chobanats*	Wild game stew
Nadjeveni pečeni šaran	*nadiyevenee pechenee sharan*	Roast stuffed carp
Fiš paprikaš	*feesh papreekash*	Spicy fish stew
Orehnjača	*orehnyacha*	Walnut roulade

Easter breakfast table

The traditional Easter Sunday feast takes in cooked ham, hard-boiled eggs, spring onions, horseradish, and a French salad of chopped veggies and eggs in mayonnaise, plus traditional baskets of coloured eggs.

Another roadside attraction

Displays of home produce line the country's verges. Stop, stretch and stock up with watermelon, wild strawberries, local cheese, honey and cider vinegar, depending on the season.

Istria

Not just blessed with a truffle gold mine (both black and white), Istrians can also pick wild asparagus and aromatic herbs wherever they turn. And rather than merely kiss under the mistletoe, they transform it into a quite delicious brandy: **biska**. Ingenious.

Signature dishes

(see the Menu decoder for more dishes)

Fuži s tartufima	*foozhee s tartoofeema*	Istrian pasta with truffle sauce
Istarska jota	*eestarska yota*	Sauerkraut, beans and meat
Istarska supa	*eestarska soopa*	Red wine, olive oil, sugar and pepper soup
Žgvacet od divljeg zeca	*zhgvatset od deevlyeg zetsa*	Wild rabbit stew
Manęštra od bobići	*maneshtra od bobeechee*	Thick bean, corn and bacon soup

Dalmatia

Croatia's best-known regional cuisine combines Mediterranean traditions and fabulous ingredients. Choose between wild-herb-infused lamb from the Kvarner islands and freshly caught sea bass or bream, deliciously prepared **na gradele** (grilled with olive oil). Pair it with **bevanda** – rich red wine mixed with water – for a delicious meal.

Signature dishes
(see the Menu decoder for more dishes)

Hobotnica ispod peke	*hobotneetsa ees-pod peke*	Octopus cooked in a **peka**
Pašticada	*pashteetsada*	Herb-braised beef
Brodet	*brodet*	Fish broth
Pršut	*pershoot*	Ham cured in the Bora wind
Smokvenjaci	*smokvenyacee*	Dried fig, walnut, **rakija** and aniseed biscuits
Paški sir	*pashkee seer*	Authentic sheep's cheese from Pag

Wine, beer & spirits

Croatians' epicurean tastes have no bounds and this applies to drink as well. Continental wines include **rizling** and **traminac**, while Dalmatian **teran** and **postup** are a must. The nation's health and spirit is kept up with the unavoidable **rakija** (strong fruit liqueur). Add herbs, walnuts, pears or honey – or just about any fruit of the earth – and it only gets better.

Šljivovicu	*shlyeevoveetsoo*	Plum schnapps
Travaricu	*travareetzu*	**Rakija** with herbs
Gemišt	*gemeesht*	White wine spritzer
Bevandu	*bevandoo*	Red wine with still water
Pelinkovac	*peleenkovats*	Strong wormwood liqueur

Sip and savour

Croats produce a fine line of liqueurs and dessert wines. Good examples are bittersweet wormwood **pelinkovac** and Samobor's spiced wine **bermet**.

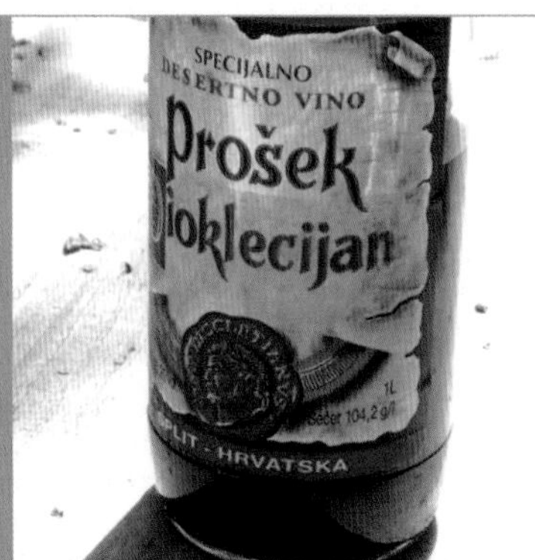

Could I have...	**Mogu li dobiti...**	*mogoo lee dobeetee...*
- a beer?	**- pivo?**	*- peevo?*
- a glass/a bottle of white/red/rosé wine?	**- čašu/bocu bijelog/crnog/roze vina?**	*- chashoo/botsoo beeyelog/tsernog/roze veena?*
- a glass/a bottle of champagne?	**- čašu/bocu šampanjca?**	*- chashoo/botsoo shampanytsa?*
- a gin and tonic?	**- gin tonik?**	*- dzheen toneek?*
- a rum and coke?	**- rum kolu?**	*- room koloo?*
- a whisky?	**- viski?**	*- veeskee?*

You may hear...

Što bi ste željeli?	*shto bee ste zhelylee?*	What can I get you?
Kako bi ste htjeli?	*kako bee ste htiyelee?*	How would you like it?
S ledom il' bez?	*s ledom eelee bez?*	With or without ice?
Hladno ili sobne temperature?	*hladno eelee sobne temperatoore?*	Cold or room temperature?

Snacks & refreshments

A 'coffee' order results in espresso, which is never drunk quickly, despite its name. Add milk for **macchiato**, or whipped cream. If you fancy a cuppa, ask for black tea – herbal teas such as rosehip and hibiscus are the alternatives. A popular local winter cure-all is black tea with lemon and rum.

Ćevapčići	*chevapcheechee*	Sausage-shaped beef/pork rissoles
Čaj s rumom	*chaiy s roomom*	Tea with rum
Tost	*tost*	Cheese and ham toasted sandwich
Kikiriki	*keekeereekee*	Peanuts
Gusti sok od breskve/marelice	*goostee sok od breskve/mareleetse*	Smooth, pulpy peach/apricot juice
Bistri sok od jabuke/borovnice	*beestree sok od yabooke/borovneetse*	Clear apple/blueberry juice
Meze	*meze*	Olives, cheeses, cured meats and/or pickles

Vegetarians & special requirements

I'm vegetarian	**Ja sam...**	*ya sam...*
	- vegetarijanac *m*	*- vegetareeyanats*
	- vegetarijanka *f*	*- vegetareeanka*
I don't eat...	**Ne jedem...**	*ne yedem...*
- meat	**- meso**	*- meso*
- fish	**- ribu**	*- reeboo*
Could you cook something without meat in it?	**Možete li pripremiti nešto bez mesa?**	*mozhete lee preepremeetee neshto bez mesa?*
What's in this?	**Koji su sastojci?**	*koyee soo sastoytsee?*
I'm allergic to...	**Patim od alergije na...**	*pateem od alerge-eye na...*
- nuts	**- koštunjavo voće**	*- koshtoonyavo voche*
- wheat	**- pšenicu**	*- pshenitzoo*
- dairy	**- mlijeko i mliječne proizvode**	*- mleeyeko ee mleeyechne proeezvode*

Children

Are children welcome?	**Mogu li djeca slobodno ući?**	*mogoo lee diyetsa slobodno oochee?*
Do you have a children's menu?	**Imate li dječji jelovnik?**	*eemate lee diyetsi-yee yelovneek?*
What dishes are good for children?	**Što preporučujete za djecu?**	*shto preporoo-chooyete za diyetsoo?*

Eco and Agrotourism

Experience farm-fresh food – and a warm welcome – at the source. These places are exceptionally child-friendly, too. Organic farm Zrno near Zagreb and Ravlic Agrotourism in Lonjsko Polje National Park are tried, tested and wonderful.

Menu decoder

Essentials

English	Croatian	Pronunciation
Breakfast	**Doručak**	*doroochak*
Lunch	**Ručak**	*roochak*
Dinner	**Večera**	*vechera*
VAT inclusive	**PDV uključen**	*pay day vay ookliyoochen*
Service included	**Usluga uključena**	*ooslooga ookliy-oochena*
Credit cards (not) accepted	**(Ne) primaju se kreditne kartice**	*(ne) preemayoo se kredeetne karteetse*
First course	**Predjelo**	*prediyelo*
Second course	**Glavno jelo**	*glavno yelo*
Dessert	**Slastice**	*slasteetse*
Dish of the day	**Dnevna ponuda**	*dnevna ponooda*
House specials	**Specijaliteti kuće**	*spetseeyaleetetee kooche*
Set menu	**Dnevni jelovnik**	*dnevnee yelovneek*
A la carte menu	**Jelovnik a la carte**	*yelovneek a la carte*
Tourist menu	**Turistički jelovnik**	*tooreesteechkee yelovneek*
Wine list	**Vinska karta**	*veenska karta*
Drinks menu	**Cjenik pića**	*tsiyeneek peecha*
Snack menu	**Zakuske**	*zakooske*
Buffet	**Švedski stol**	*shvedskee stol*

Methods of preparation

English	Croatian	Pronunciation
Baked	**Pečeno**	*pecheno*
Boiled	**Kuhano**	*koohano*
Braised	**Pirjano (dinstano)**	*peeriyano (deen-stano)*
Breaded	**Pohano**	*pohano*
Deep-fried	**Prženo u dubokom ulju**	*perzheno oo doobokom oolyoo*
Fresh	**Svježe**	*sviyezhe*
Fried	**Prženo**	*perzheno*
Frozen	**Smrznuto**	*smerzhnooto*
Grilled/broiled	**S roštilja/na gradele**	*s roshteelya/na gradele*
Marinated	**Marinirano**	*mareeneerano*

Food for the soul

Where there is nourishment, song will soon follow. It's not uncommon for groups of drinkers and diners – male and female – to burst into impromptu melody. In Dalmatia you may be lucky and dine in the company of a **klapa**, traditional male acapella choir.

Mashed	**Pire**	*peere*
Poached	**Poširano**	*posheerano*
Raw	**Sirovo**	*seerovo*
Roasted	**Pečeno**	*pecheno*
Salty	**Slano**	*slano*
Sautéed	**Prženo 'na naglo'**	*perzheno na naglo*
Smoked	**Dimljeno**	*deemlyeno*
Spicy (flavour)	**Jako začinjeno**	*yako zacheenyeno*
Spicy (hot)	**Ljuto**	*lyooto*
Steamed	**Kuhano na pari**	*koohano na paree*
Stewed	**Pirjano**	*peeriyano*
Stuffed	**Punjeno**	*poonyeno*
Sweet	**Slatko**	*slatko*

Rare	**Slabo pečeno**	*slabo pecheno*
Medium	**Srednje pečeno**	*srednyea pecheno*
Well done	**Dobro pečeno**	*dobro pecheno*

Common food items

Beef	**Govedina/junetina**	*govedeena/yoone-teena*
Chicken	**Piletina**	*peeleteena*
Turkey	**Puretina**	*pooreteena*
Lamb	**Janjetina**	*yanyeteena*
Pork	**Svinjetina**	*sveenyeteena*
Veal	**Teletina**	*teleteena*

Fish	**Riba**	*reeba*
Seafood	**Plodovi mora**	*plodovee mora*
Tuna	**Tunjevina**	*toonyeveena*
Beans	**Grah**	*grah*
Cheese	**Sir**	*seer*
Eggs	**Jaja**	*yaiya*
Lentils	**Leća**	*lecha*
Pasta/noodles	**Tjestenina/rezanci**	*tiyesteneena/rezantsee*
Rice	**Riža**	*reezha*
Cabbage	**Kupus**	*koopoos*
Carrots	**Mrkva**	*merkva*
Cucumber	**Krastavac**	*krastavats*
Garlic	**Češnjak**	*cheshnyak*
Mushrooms	**Gljive**	*glyeeve*
Olives	**Masline**	*masleene*
Onion	**Luk**	*look*
Potato	**Krumpir**	*kroompeer*
Red/green pepper	**Crvena/zelena paprika**	*cervena/zelena papreeka*
Tomato	**Rajčica**	*raycheetsa*
Vegetables	**Povrće**	*poverche*
Bread	**Kruh**	*krooh*
Oil	**Ulje**	*ooilye*
Pepper	**Papar**	*papar*
Salt	**Sol**	*sol*
Vinegar	**Ocat**	*otsat*
Cake	**Kolač**	*kolach*
Cereal	**Žitarice/pahuljice**	*zheetareetse/pahoo-lyeetse*

Snuffling truffles

Notoriously difficult to gather, truffles – pungent fungi growing near the roots of oak trees – were traditionally hunted by pigs. Dogs, however, are easier to train – most importantly, they have no appetite for the bounty.

Cream	**Vrhnje**	*verhnye*
Fruit	**Voće**	*voche*
Ice-cream	**Sladoled**	*sladoled*
Milk	**Mlijeko**	*mliyeko*
Tart	**Pita**	*peeta*

Olive Oyl
Kings, newborns and the dying have been anointed with it for centuries. In Dalmatia, many locals sell their quality oil to tourists, so don't miss out.

Popular sauces

Tartar umak	*tartar oomak*	Tartar sauce
Umak od (divljih) gljiva	*oomak od (deevly-eeh) glyeeva*	(Wild) mushroom sauce
Umak od komorača	*oomak od komoracha*	Fennel sauce
Bolognese	*bolognese*	Bolognese sauce
Milanese	*milanese*	Tomato ragout
Šalša	*shalsha*	Fresh tomato sauce
Umak od Gorgonzole	*oomak od gorgonzole*	Gorgonzola sauce

First course dishes

Štrukli u juhi	*shtrooklee oo yoohee*	Soup with pastry dumplings
Krem juha od gljiva	*krem yooha od glyeeva*	Cream of mushroom soup
Goveđa juha s domaćim rezancima	*goveja jooha s domacheem rezantseema*	Beef soup with homemade noodles
Dagnje na buzaru	*dagnye na booza-roo*	Mussels, garlic, parsley and wine
Slane srdele	*slane serdele*	Salted pilchards
Salata od hobotnice	*salata od hobot-neetse*	Octopus salad
Kamenice	*kameneetse*	Oysters

Eat on the street

Each season has its street food. In late summer, the aroma of roasted sweetcorn waltzes the streets of continental Croatia. In autumn, stands begin roasting chestnuts instead.

(Mesna/vegetarijanska) plata	*(mesna/vegetareeyanska) plata*	(Meat/vegetarian) platter
Sir i pršut	*seer ee pershoot*	Cheese and Bora-wind-cured ham
Rižoto	*reezhoto*	Risotto
- s (divljim) gljivama	*- s (deevlyeem) glyeevama*	- (wild) mushroom
- s povrćem	*- s poverchem*	- vegetable
Tjestenina	*tiyesteneena*	Pasta
- karbonara	*- karbonara*	- carbonara
- sa šparogama	*- sa shparogama*	- with asparagus
Sir i vrhnje	*seer ee verhnje*	Cottage cheese and sour cream
Pohane bukovače	*pohane bookovache*	Battered oyster mushrooms
Njoki u umaku od Gorgonzole	*nyokee oo oomakoo od gorgonzole*	Gnocchi in Gorgonzola sauce
Ražnjići	*razhnychee*	Pork shish kebab

Second course dishes

Zubatac	*zoobatats*	Dentex
Brancin	*brantseen*	Sea bass
Škarpina	*shkarpeena*	Grouper
Orada	*orada*	Gilthead sea bream
Lignje pržene/pohane/na žaru	*leegnye perzhene/pohane/na zharoo*	Fried/breaded/grilled squid
Bijeli rižoto (s plodovima mora)	*beeyelee reezhoto (s plodoveema mora)*	Creamy seafood risotto
Pastrva na žaru	*pastrva na zharoo*	Grilled rainbow trout
Bečki odrezak	*bechkee odrezak*	Vienna schnitzel
Pariški odrezak	*pareeshkee odrezak*	Parisian schnitzel

Teleća koljenica ispod peke	*telecha kolyeneetsa eespod peke*	Veal shank cooked in a **peka** oven
Miješano meso	*meeyeshano meso*	Mixed grill
Gulaš (od divljači)	*goolash (od deevly-achee)*	(Wild game) goulash
- srneći	*- sernechee*	- with venison
- od divljeg zeca	*- od deevlyeg zetsa*	- with wild rabbit
- od vepra	*- od vepra*	- with wild boar
- svinjski	*- sveenyskee*	- with pork
Kotlovina	*kotloveena*	Braised pork and potatoes
Pastrva	*pastrva*	Rainbow trout
Punjene lignje	*punyene leegnye*	Stuffed squid
Krvavice	*krvaveece*	Black pudding

Side dishes

Rizi bizi	*reezee beezee*	Rice and peas
Pomfritt	*pomfritt*	French fries
Riža	*reezha*	Rice
Blitva na lešo	*bleetva na lesho*	Swiss chard, garlic, olive oil
Restani krumpir	*restanee kroom-peer*	Rough mashed, sautéed potatoes
Kuhani krumpir	*koohanee kroom-peer*	Boiled potatoes
Krumpir pire	*kroompeer peere*	Mashed potatoes
Pohani šampinjoni	*pohanee shampee-nyonee*	Breaded button mushrooms
Pohane tikvice	*pohane teekveetse*	Breaded courgette
Mlinci	*mleentsee*	Croatian pasta
Zelena salata	*zelena salata*	Green salad
Mješana salata	*miyeshana salata*	Mixed salad
Salata od…	*salata od...*	Fresh... salad
- zelenog kupusa	*- zelenog koopoosa*	- white cabbage
- crvenog kupusa	*- tservenog koopoosa*	- red cabbage
- kiselog kupusa	*- keeselog koopoosa*	- sauerkraut
Grah slata	*grah salata*	Bean salad
Salata od mahuna	*salata od mahoona*	Green bean salad
Lovačke okruglice (sa špekom)	*lovachke okroogleece (sa shpekom)*	'Hunter's dumplings' made from bread and bacon

Gravče na tavče	*gravche na tavche*	Oven-baked beans, paprika, onion, bay
Žganci	*zhgancee*	Polenta

Desserts

Rožata	*rozhata*	Crème caramel
Makovnjača	*makovnyacha*	Poppyseed roulade
(Štrudl) Savijača od...	*(shtroodl) saveey-acha od...*	... strudel
- jabuka	*- yabooka*	- Apple
- sira	*- seera*	- Cottage cheese
- višanja	*- veeshanya*	- Cherry
Bučnica	*boochneetsa*	- Pumpkin
Kremšnita	*kremshneeta*	Cream cake
Fritule	*freetoole*	Fritters
Palačinke s...	*palacheenke s...*	Pancakes with...
- pekmezom	*- pekmezom*	- jam
- orasima	*- oraseema*	- chopped walnuts
- čokoladom	*- chokoladom*	- chocolate
Međimurska gibanica	*mejeemoorska geebaneetsa*	Walnut, cheese, poppyseed and apple cake
Sladoled	*sladoled*	Ice cream
Kuglof	*kooglof*	Gugelhupf cake
Kesten pire sa šlagom	*kesten peere sa shlagom*	Chestnut with whipped cream
Okruglice sa šljivama	*okroogleece sa shlyeevama*	Plum dumplings

We all scream

Glorious ice cream... Croatia's favourite. The national family pastime is an excursion for a cold treat. Choice is good, varied and fresh, often reflecting an Italian gelato influence.

Drinks

Gazirana mineralna voda	*gazeerana meener-alna voda*	Sparkling mineral water
Negazirana mineralna voda	*negazeerana meen-eralna voda*	Still mineral water

A grape journey

Zinfandel – long considered California's indigenous grape – is, in fact, Croatian. In 2002, scientists at UC Davis discovered its genetic code is identical to a local strain.

Prirodni (voćni) sokovi	*preerodnee (vochnee) sokovee*	Fresh (fruit) juices
Gusti sokovi	*goostee sokovee*	Smooth pulpy juices
Bistri sokovi	*beestree sokovee*	Clear juices
Kava sa šlagom	*kava sa shlagom*	Coffee with cream
Vruća čokolada	*vroocha chokolada*	Hot chocolate
Macchiato	*makeeato*	Espresso with milk
Bermet	*bermet*	Spiced wine
Prošek	*proshek*	Red dessert wine
Medovina	*medoveena*	Mead
Gvirc	*gveerts*	Spiced mead
Rakija	*rakeeya*	Croatian schnapps
Medovača	*medovacha*	**Rakija** with honey
Rakija od rogača	*rakeeya od rogacha*	**Rakija** with carob
Višnjevača	*veeshnyevacha*	Cherry **rakija**
Viljamovka	*veelyamovka*	Pear **rakija**
Šljivovica	*shlyeevoveetsa*	Plum **rakija**
Loza	*loza*	Grape **rakija**
Travarica	*travareetsa*	**Rakija** with herbs
Biska	*beeska*	**Rakija** with mistletoe
Orahovica/ orahovača	*orahoveetsa/oraho-vacha*	**Rakija** with walnuts
Ožujsko pivo	*oshooysko peevo*	Beer brewed in Zagreb
Karlovačko pivo	*karlovachko peevo*	Beer brewed in Karlovac

Snacks

Čips	*cheeps*	Crisps
Sendvič	*sendveech*	Sandwich
Topli sendvič	*toplee sendveech*	Hot sandwich
Livanjski sir	*leevanyskee seer*	Cheese from Livno
Kozji sir	*koziyee seer*	Goat's cheese
Masline	*masleene*	Olives

Shopping

Cities have many small boutiques with long opening hours, selling design jewellery, antique wares and local delicacies. Mushrooming shopping centres promote a mix of Croatian and international outlets. Stores and supermarkets often stay open from 7am until 9pm, but Sunday working hours are short or nonexistent. The coast and islands have a siesta culture, shuttering down for the afternoon. The Konzum chain usually has self-service, but otherwise be prepared to order in Croatian. DM equates with Boots, very handy for cosmetics, toiletries and nappies.

Essentials

English	Croatian	Pronunciation
Where can I buy...?	**Gdje mogu kupiti…?**	*gdyea mogoo koopeetee...?*
I'd like to buy...	**Želim kupiti…**	*zheleem koopee-tee...*
Do you have...?	**Imate li…?**	*eemate lee...?*
Do you sell...?	**Prodajete li…?**	*prodaiyete lee...?*
I'd like this	**Molim Vas ovo**	*moleem vas ovo*
I'd prefer...	**Više bi mi odgovaralo…**	*veeshe bee mee odgovaralo...*
Could you show me...?	**Možete li mi pokazati…?**	*mozhete lee mee pokazatee...?*
I'm just looking, thanks	**Samo gledam, hvala**	*samo gledam, hvala*
How much is it?	**Koliko ovo košta?**	*koleeko ovo koshta?*
Could you write down the price?	**Možete li mi napisati cijenu?**	*mozhete lee mee napeesatee tseeyenoo?*
Do you have any items on sale?	**Imate li nešto na rasprodaji?**	*eemate lee neshto na rasprodaiyee?*
Could I have a discount?	**Mogu li dobiti popust?**	*mogoo lee dobeetee popoost?*
Nothing else, thanks	**To je sve, hvala**	*to ye sve, hvala*
Do you accept credit cards?	**Primate li kreditne kartice?**	*preemate lee kre-deetne karteetse?*
It's a present, could I have it wrapped, please?	**Ovo je poklon, možete li mi zamotati?**	*ovo ye poklon, mozhete lee mee zamotatee?*
Could you post it to...?	**Možete li ovo poslati na…?**	*mozhete lee ovo poslatee na...?*
Can I exchange it?	**Mogu li ovo zamijeniti?**	*mogoo lee ovo zameeyeneetee?*
I'd like to return this	**Želim ovo vratiti**	*zheleem ovo vrateetee*
I'd like a refund	**Možete li mi vratiti novce?**	*mozhete lee mee vrateetee novtse?*

Local specialities

Each region has its specialties, but Croatia is a small country: if you forgot to buy truffle products in Istria, you will most certainly be able to pick some up in Zagreb.

Can you recommend a shop selling local specialities?	**Možete li preporučiti dućan koji prodaje lokalne specijalitete?**	*mozhete lee pre-poroocheetee doochan koyee prodayea lokalne spetseeyaleetete?*
What are the local specialities?	**Koji su lokalni specijaliteti?**	*koyee soo lokalnee spetseeyaleetetee?*
Is... (leather) good quality?	**Je li… (koža) dobre kvalitete?**	*ye lee... (kozha) dobre kvaleetete?*
Do you make the... (ceramics) yourself?	**Izrađujete li sami… (keramiku)?**	*eezrajooyete lee sami... (kerameekoo)?*
Is it hand made?	**Je li ovo ručni rad?**	*ye lee ovo roochnee rad?*
Do you make it to measure?	**Pravite li ovo po mjeri?**	*praveete lee ovo po miyeree?*
Can I order one?	**Mogu li naručiti jedan/jednu** *m/f* **?**	*mogoo lee naroocheetee yedan/yednoo?*

Hrvat Croat, Cravat Tie

...is pretty much how it went. The French loved the colourful scarves that Croat soldiers wore as they rolled into Paris in 1635. They named the style "a la Croat," which changed to "cravat" and endured.

Popular things to buy

Licitarsko srce	*leetseetarsko sertse*	Traditional, red dough Licitar heart
Hrvatski pleter	*hervatskee pleter*	Traditional Croatian knotwork
Paška čipka	*pashka cheepka*	Lace from Pag island

Bank holiday bonanza

Croats benefit from at least 14 public holidays, so there's a good chance you'll run into one. Shops don't stay open just for tourists, so check at www.timeanddate.com/calendar.

Paški sir	*pashkee seer*	Cheese from Pag island
Koraljni nakit	*koralynee nakeet*	Coral jewellery
Filigran	*feeleegran*	Filigree silver
Hvarsko lavandino ulje	*hervatsko lavan-deeno oolyea*	Lavender oil from Hvar island
Ulje od tartufa	*oolyea od tartoofa*	Truffle oil
Maslinovo ulje	*masleenovo oolyea*	Olive oil
Rakija	*rakeeya*	Fruit schnapps
Pršut	*pershoot*	Bora-wind-cured ham
Vino	*veeno*	Wine
Moretto nakit	*moretto nakeet*	Moretto jewellery
Prirodna kozmetika	*preerodna kozme-teeka*	Natural cosmetics
Antikni predmeti	*anteeknee predme-tee*	Antiques

Clothes & shoes

Croatians like to dress well and their standards are high, especially when it comes to shoes (a trait shared with their Italian neighbours). Zagreb's Kaptol shopping centre is a great one to visit, not least for its lovely location.

Where is the... department?	**Gdje je odjel...**	*gdiye ye odiyel...*
- clothes	**- konfekcije?**	*- konfektseeye?*
- shoe	**- obuće?**	*- obooche?*

- women's	**- ženske odjeće?**	*- zhenske odiyeche?*
- men's	**- muške odjeće?**	*- mooshke odiyeche?*
- children's	**- dječje odjeće?**	*- diyechiye odiyeche?*
Which floor is the...?	**Na kojem je katu…?**	*na koyem ye katoo...?*
I'm looking for...	**Tražim…**	*trazheem...*
- a skirt	**- suknju**	*- sooknyoo*
- trousers	**- hlače**	*- hlache*
- a top	**- majicu**	*- maiyeetsoo*
- a jacket	**- jaknu**	*- yaknoo*
- a T-shirt	**- majicu kratkih rukava**	*- maiyeetsoo krat-keeh rookava*
- jeans	**- traperice**	*- trapereetse*
- shoes	**- cipele**	*- tseepele*
- underwear	**- donje rublje**	*- donye rooblye*
Can I try it on?	**Mogu li probati?**	*mogoo lee proba-tee?*
What size is it?	**Koja je ovo veličina?**	*koya ye ovo veleecheena?*
My size is...	**Moja veličina je…**	*moya veleecheena ye...*
- small	**- small**	*- smol*
- medium	**- medium**	*- meedyoom*
- large	**- large**	*- larch*

(see clothes size converter on p.96 for full range of sizes)

Truffle buff

Giancarlo Zigante is Istria's Mr Truffle. He lays claim to the biggest truffle ever found, a 1.3kg monster, and his shops sell everything from white truffles to truffled sheep cheese. See www.zigantetartufi.com.

Do you have this in my size?	**Imate li ovo u mom broju?**	*eemate lee ovo oo mom broyoo?*
Where is the changing room?	**Gdje je svlačionica?**	*gdiye je svalacheeoneetsa?*
It doesn't fit	**Nije mi dobro**	*neeye mee dobro*
It doesn't suit me	**Ne pristaje mi**	*ne preestaiye mee*
Do you have a... size?	**Imate li… broj**	*eemate lee... broy*
- bigger	**- manji?**	*- manyee?*
- smaller	**- veći?**	*- vechee?*
Do you have it/them in...	**Imate li ovo… boje?**	*eemate lee ovo... boye?*
- black?	**- crne**	*- tserne*
- white?	**- bijele**	*- beeyele*
- blue?	**- plave**	*- plave*
- green?	**- zelene**	*- zelene*
- red?	**- crvene**	*- tservene*
Are they made of leather?	**Jesu li kožne?**	*yesoo lee kozhne?*
I'm going to leave it/them	**Ne uzimam**	*ne oozieemam*
I'll take it/them	**Uzimam**	*oozeemam*

You may hear...

Mogu li Vam pomoći?	*mogoo lee vam pomochee?*	Can I help you?

Naïve art

Established in the 1920s among a small group of untrained painters and sculptors, this art form has a dedicated museum in Zagreb and is on sale in workshops, galleries and souvenir shops.

Licitar hearts

Zagreb's favourite souvenir, the Licitar heart, was traditionally made from honey or gingerbread dough. Give it to your love – with love – and it all comes back to you. Don't eat.

Koje veličine?	*koye veleecheene?*	What size?
To nažalost nemamo	*to nazhalost nemamo*	We don't have any
Izvolite	*eezvoleete*	Here you are
Još nešto?	*yosh neshto?*	Anything else?
Hoću li Vam zamotati?	*hochoo lee vam zamotatee?*	Shall I wrap it for you?
To je (50) eura	*to ye (pedeset) eoora*	It's... (50) euros
Na sniženju je	*na sneezhenyoo ye*	It's reduced

Where to shop

Where can I find a...	**Gdje mogu naći...**	*gdyea mogoo nachee...*
- bookshop?	**- knjižaru?**	*- knyeezharoo?*
- clothes shop?	**- prodavaonicu odjeće?**	*- prodavaoneetsoo odiyeche?*
- department store?	**- robnu kuću?**	*- robnoo koochoo?*
- gift shop?	**- suvenirnicu?**	*- sooveneereetsoo?*
- music shop?	**- glazbenu prodavaonicu?**	*- glasbenoo prodavaonitsoo?*
- market?	**- tržnicu?**	*- terzhneetsoo?*
- newsagent?	**- kiosk s novinama?**	*- keeosk s noveena-ma?*
- shoe shop?	**- prodavaonicu cipela?**	*- prodavaonitsoo tseepela?*
- stationer's?	**- papirnicu?**	*- papeerneetsoo?*
- tobacconist?	**- tobacco?**	*- tobacco?*

- souvenir shop	**- suvenirnicu?**	*- sooveneerneetsoo?*
What's the best place to buy...?	**Gdje je najbolje kupiti…?**	*gdiyea ye naiybolye koopeetee?*
I'd like to buy...	**Želim kupiti…**	*zheleem koopeetee...*
- a film	**- film**	*- feelm*
- an English newspaper	**- novine na engleskom**	*- noveene na engleskom*
- a map/city map	**- kartu/plan grada**	*- kartoo/plan grada*
- postcards	**- razglednicu**	*- razgledneetsoo*
- a present	**- poklon**	*- poklon*
- stamps	**- marke**	*- marke*
- sun cream	**- kremu za sunčanje**	*- kremoo za soon-chanyea*

Three for a fiver

Most towns have a colourful food market, usually open daily (except Sundays) between 8am and 2pm. A must for self-caterers, but also a good insight into local eating habits.

Food & markets

Is there a supermarket/ market nearby?	**Je li blizu supermarket/ prodavaonica?**	*ye lee bleezoo soopermarket/ prodavaoneetsa?*
Can I have...	**Mogu li dobiti…**	*mogoo lee dobee-tee...*
- some bread?	**- kruha?**	*- krooha?*
- some fruit?	**- voća?**	*- vocha?*
- some cheese?	**- sira?**	*- seera?*
- a bottle of water?	**- bocu vode?**	*- botsoo vode?*
- a bottle of wine?	**- bocu vina?**	*- botsoo veena?*
I'd like... of that	**Molim Vas… ovoga**	*moleem vas... ovoga*
- half a kilo	**- pola kile**	*- pola keele*
- 250 grams	**- 250 grama**	*- 250 grama*
- a small/big piece	**- mali/veliki komad**	*- malee/veleekee komad*

Getting around

Communication and connection sit comfortably here, beside all those wonderful traditions. Frequent flights link the coast and the capital Zagreb, as no-frill airlines boom. Fly direct to your destination or, for more freedom, journey down the Adriatic Highway connecting Rijeka and Dubrovnik, the most picturesque route in Croatia. Car rental is fairly straightforward – and is usually conducted in English, if need be. Meet the locals on a bus or get windswept on a ferry, while trains link the country to its neighbours.

Arrival

Croatian airports come in two sizes: small and smaller. The terminals aren't luxurious, but cover essentials such as a money exchange, car hire, tourist information and refreshments. Any taxi ride from the airport is likely to be expensive, so explore other options.

Where...	**Gdje...**	*gdyea...*
- is the luggage from flight...?	**- je prtljaga s leta...?**	*- ye pertliyaga s leta...?*
- are the luggage trolleys?	**- su kolica za prtljagu?**	*- soo koleetsa za pertliyagoo?*
- is the lost luggage office?	**- je ured za izgubljenu prtljagu?**	*- ye oored za eezgoobliyenoo pertliyagoo?*

Where...	**Gdje...**	*gdyea...*
- are the buses?	**- su autobusi?**	*- soo aootoboosee?*
- are the trains?	**- su vlakovi?**	*- soo vlakovee?*
- are the taxis?	**- su taksiji?**	*- soo takseeyee?*
- is the car rental?	**- je rent-a-car?**	*- ye rent-a-car?*
- is the exit?	**- je izlaz?**	*- ye eezlaz?*
How do I get to hotel...?	**Kako mogu doći do hotela...?**	*kako mogoo dochee do hotela?*

My baggage is...	**Moja prtljaga je...**	*moya pertliyaga ye...*
- lost	**- izgubljena**	*- eezgoobliyena*
- damaged	**- oštećena**	*- oshtechena*
- stolen	**- ukradena**	*- ookradena*

Customs

The somewhat humourless officials are more likely to wave visitors through than frisk them. Duty is not payable on personal belongings, and foreign currency can be imported and exported freely.

The children are on this passport	**Djeca su na ovoj putovnici**	*diyetsa soo na ovoy pootovneetsee*
We're here on holiday	**Došli smo na odmor**	*doshlee smo na odmor*
I'm going to...	**Putujem u...**	*pootooyem oo...*

I have nothing to declare	**Nemam ništa za prijaviti**	*nemam neeshta za preeyaveetee*
Do I have to declare this?	**Moram li ovo prijaviti?**	*moram lee ovo preeyaveetee?*

Car hire

Most companies in airports or resorts accept full British driving licenses for cars and scooters. Choose known names – such as Hertz, Avis and Budget – or contact tourist information offices and check on-line for local alternatives.

I'd like to hire a...	**Želim unajmiti...**	*zheleem oo-naiymeetee...*
- car	**- auto**	*- aooto*
- people carrier	**- monovolumen**	*- monovoloomen*
with...	**s...**	*s...*
- air conditioning	**- klimom**	*- kleemom*
- automatic transmission	**- automatskim mjenjačem**	*- aootomatskeem miyenyachem*

Pay and display by SMS

Text your registration number to 101 (red parking zone), 102 (yellow zone), or 103 (green zone) to extend your parking permit without leaving the table, beach or bed.

How much is that for a...	**Pošto je najam za...**	*poshto ye naiyam za...*
- day?	**- jedan dan?**	*- yedan dan?*
- week?	**- tjedan dana?**	*- tiyedan dana?*
Does that include...	**Uključuje li cijena...**	*ookliyoochooye lee tseeyena...*
- mileage?	**- kilometražu?**	*- keelomtrazhoo?*
- insurance?	**- osiguranje?**	*- oseeguranye?*

On the road

Driving grants the best vistas and happy adventures. Switch on the low-beam lights at all times, obey speed limits and be informed – for example, a yellow traffic light means 'don't go'. Croatia is a zero-tolerance region: never drink alcohol and drive. Also, watch for abrupt, barely signed border crossings and speed-limit shifts.

What is the speed limit?	**Koje je ograničenje brzine?**	*koye ye ograneechenye berzeene?*
Can I park here?	**Mogu li ovdje parkirati?**	*mogoo lee ovdiyea parkeeratee?*
Where is a petrol station?	**Gdje je benzinska postaja?**	*gdyea ye benzeenska postaiya?*
Please fill up the tank with...	**Molim Vas… gorivo**	*moleem vas... goree-vo*
- unleaded	**- bezolovno**	*- bezolovno*
- diesel	**- dizel**	*- deezel*
- leaded	**- normalno**	*- normalno*
- LPG	**- auto-plin**	*- aooto-pleen*

Directions

Is this the road to...?	**Je li ovo cesta za…?**	*ye lee ovo tsesta za...?*
How do I get to...?	**Kako mogu doći do…?**	*kako mogoo dochee do...?*
How far is it to...?	**Koliko je daleko…?**	*koleeko ye daleko...?*
How long will it take to...?	**Koliko je vremena do…?**	*koleeko ye vremena do...?*
Could you point it out on the map?	**Možete li mi pokazati na karti?**	*mozhete lee mee pokazatee na kartee?*
I've lost my way	**Izgubljen/a** *m/f* **sam**	*eezgoobliyen/eezgoo bliyena sam*
On the right/left	**S desna/lijeva**	*s desna/leeyeva*
Turn right/left	**Skrenite desno/lijevo**	*skreneetee desno/leeyevo*
Straight ahead	**Ravno**	*ravno*
Turn around	**Okrenite se**	*okreneete se*

Public transport

Avoid driving hassles with the bus, train and Zagreb's tram. These ecologically friendly services continue late into the night. Tickets can be bought at newspaper kiosks or from the driver for a couple of kunas more. A day pass in the capital is 19 kn.

Bus	**Autobus**	*aootoboos*
Bus station	**Autobusni kolodvor**	*aootoboosnee kolo-dvor*
Train	**Vlak**	*vlak*
Train station	**Kolodvor**	*kolodvor*

Funny funicular

Zagreb's funicular is one of the world's shortest at just 66 metres. The swift, steep ascent connects central Ilica Street with the upper town.

I would like to go to...	**Želim putovati u...**	*zheleem pootovatee oo...*
I would like a...	**Molim Vas...**	*moleem vas...*
- single ticket	**- kartu u jednom smjeru**	*- kartoo oo yednom smiyeroo*
- return ticket	**- povratnu kartu**	*- povratnoo kartoo*
- first class ticket	**- kartu za prvi razred**	*- kartoo za pervee razred*
- smoking/non-smoking ticket	**- kartu za pušačko/ nepušačko mjesto**	*- kartoo za pooshachko/nepoo-shachko miyesto*
What time does it leave/arrive?	**Kada polazimo/ stižemo?**	*kada polazimo/ steezhemo?*
Could you tell me when to get off?	**Možete li mi reći gdje da siđem?**	*mozhete lee mee rechee gdyea da seejem?*

Taxis

I'd like a taxi to...	**Molim Vas taksi do...**	*moleem vas taksee do...*
How much is it to the...	**Koliko košta vožnja do...**	*koleeko koshta vozh-nya do...*
- airport?	**- zračne luke?**	*- zrachne looke?*
- town centre?	**- centra?**	*- tsentra?*
- hotel?	**- hotela?**	*- hotela?*

Tours

Croatian tours offer an increasingly wide menu, from city treasures, wine tasting and island hopping, to guided adventures and doing time on the equivalent of Alcatraz: Goli otok, near Rab. Most are available in English.

Are there any organised tours of the town/region?	**Ima li organiziranih obilazaka grada/ regije?**	*eema lee orga-neezeeraneeh obeelazaka grada/ regeeye?*
Where do they leave from?	**S kojeg mjesta kreću?**	*s koyeg miyesta kre-choo?*
What time does it start?	**Kada se kreće?**	*kada se kreche?*
Do you have English-speaking guides?	**Imate li vodiče koji govore engleski?**	*eemate lee vodeeche koyee govore engleskee?*
Is lunch included?	**Je li ručak uključen u cijenu?**	*ye lee roochak oo-kliyoochen oo tseeyenoo?*
Is tea included?	**Je li večera uključena u cijenu?**	*ye lee verchera oo-kliyoochena oo tseeyenoo?*
Do we get any free time?	**Imamo li slobodno vrijeme?**	*eemamo lee slobo-dno vreeyeme?*
Are we going to see...?	**Hoćemo li posjetiti…?**	*hochemo lee poseeyeteetee...?*
What time do we get back?	**Kad se vraćamo?**	*kad se vrachamo?*

I spy… a church on a hill

Worshippers built churches on the highest ground – to suffer the tough ascent was to bring the faithful ever closer to God. Prettily lit chapels still look phenomenal on night-time jaunts.

Accommodation

For decades, Croatians welcomed tourists to hotels – or, more often, directly under their roofs. The coast was especially hospitable, with almost every home renting rooms or mother-in-law flats during the high seasons. Now innovation is the order of the day; visitors can enjoy barns, tepees, castles, Robinson islands, macrobiotic farms, luxury villas and even lighthouses. Istria is a very fine example of sustainable, imaginative tourism. Many properties now offer activities like gliding, rafting, diving, fishing, horse riding, cave exploring and wine tasting.

Types of accommodation

"Zimmer, camera, rooms," shout the signs outside many houses. The distinctions are sometimes blurred: not all apartments are self-contained, for example. Some share a terrace table with the owners (no bad thing, really). Also ask about breakfast, which is not always included in the price. Villas and whole-house rentals are usually self-catering.

I'd like to stay in...	**Želim odsjesti u…**	*zheleem odsyestee oo...*
- an apartment	**- apartmanu**	*- apartmanoo*
- a campsite	**- kampu**	*- kampoo*
- a hotel	**- hotelu**	*- hoteloo*
- a youth hostel	**- hostelu**	*- hosteloo*
- a guest house	**- pansionu**	*- panseeonoo*
Is it...	**Je li to…**	*ye lee to...*
- full board?	**- puni pansion?**	*- poonee panseeon?*
- half board?	**- polupansion?**	*- poloopanseeon?*
- self-catering?	**- apartmanska ponuda?**	*- apartmanska ponooda?*

Light in the night

Surely a lighthouse in the middle of the Adriatic is the very spirit of romantic seclusion. The website www.adriatica.net lists island getaways, along with yacht rentals and more traditional accommodation.

Reservations

Do you have any rooms available?	**Imate li slobodnih soba?**	*eemate lee slobodneeh soba?*
Can you recommend anywhere else?	**Možete li mi preporučiti negdje drugdje?**	*mozhete lee mee preporoocheetee negdiye droogdiye?*

I'd like to make a reservation for...	**Želim rezervaciju za...**	*zheleem rezervatseeyoo za...*
- tonight	**- večeras**	*- vecheras*
- one night	**- jednu noć**	*- yednoo noch*
- two nights	**- dvije noći**	*- dveeyea nochee*
- a week	**- tjedan dana**	*- tiyedan dana*
From... (May 1st) to... (May 8th)	**Od... (1. svibnja) do... (8. svibnja)**	*od... (pervog sveebnya) do... (osmog sveebnya)*

Room types

Most hotels offer standard amenities, but gorgeous views are often a perk that pads the price. Double rooms may, in fact, be twins. Request a French bed, **francuski krevet** (*francooskee krevet*), for a more romantic and comfortable experience. Bathrooms are commonly equipped with a shower, rather then a bath.

Do you have... room?	**Imate li... sobu?**	*eemate lee... soboo?*
- a single	**- jednokrevetnu**	*- yednokrevetnoo*
- a double	**- dvokrevetnu**	*- dvokrevetnoo*
- a family	**- obiteljsku**	*- obeeteliyskoo*
with...	**s...**	*s...*
- a cot?	**- dječjim krevetom?**	*- diyechyeem krevetom?*
- twin beds?	**- dva kreveta?**	*- dva kreveta?*
- a double bed?	**- francuskim krevetom?**	*- frantsooskeem krevetom?*
- a bath/shower?	**- kupaonicom/ tušem?**	*- koopaoneetsom/ tooshem?*
- air-conditioning?	**- klimom?**	*- kleemom?*
- internet access?	**- internetom?**	*- eenternetom?*
Can I see the room?	**Mogu li vidjeti sobu?**	*mogoo lee veediyetee soboo?*

Prices

Prices vary throughout the year, reaching their highest level in July and August. Rates almost halve in spring, autumn and winter. Some properties add accommodation tax – approximately 10 kuna per person – to the bill, and extra heating charges sometimes apply in winter.

How much is...	**Koliko košta...**	*koleeko koshta...*
- a room for two people?	**- soba za dvoje?**	*- soba za dvoyea?*
- per night?	**- za jednu noć?**	*- za yednoo noch?*
- per week?	**- za tjedan dana?**	*- za tiyedan dana?*
Is breakfast included?	**Je li doručak uključen u cijenu?**	*ye lee doroochak ookliyoochen oo tseeyenoo?*
Do you have a reduction for children?	**Imate li popust za djecu?**	*eemate lee popoost za diyetsoo?*
Do you have a single room supplement?	**Naplaćujete li ekstra za jednu osobu?**	*naplachooyete lee ekstra za yednoo osoboo?*
Is there...	**Ima li (hotel)...**	*eema lee (hotel)...*
- a swimming pool?	**- bazen?**	*- bazen?*
- an elevator?	**- dizalo?**	*- deezalo?*
I'll take it	**Pristajem**	*preestayem*
Can I pay by...	**Mogu li platiti...**	*mogoo li plateetee...*
- credit card?	**- kreditnom karticom?**	*- kredeetnom karteetsom?*
- traveller's cheque?	**- putničkim čekovima?**	*- pootneechkeem chekoveema?*

Sleep in the park

A national park, that is. Croatia offers a variety of places to stay among the mountains, lakes and waterfalls of its many national parks, from camping to luxury villas.

Special requests

Could you...	**Možete li...**	*mozhete lee...*
- put this in the hotel safe?	**- staviti ovo u hotelski sef?**	*- staveetee ovo oo hotelskee sef?*

Five a day

Snackers and self-caterers should shop at farmers' markets. Explore Zagreb's Dolac, if only for the wonderful atmosphere. The lucky few may even have their own veggie patches included in their accommodation.

- order a taxi for me?	**- mi naručiti taksi?**	*- mee naroocheetee taksee?*
- wake me up at (7am)?	**- me probuditi u (7 ujutro)?**	*- me proboodeetee oo (sedam oo-yootro)?*
Can I have a room with a sea view?	**Mogu li dobiti sobu s pogledom na more?**	*mogoo lee dobee-tee soboo s pogledom na more?*
Can I have...	**Mogu li dobiti…**	*mogoo lee dobee-tee...*
- a bigger room?	**- veću sobu?**	*- vechoo soboo?*
- a quieter room?	**- tišu sobu?**	*- teeshoo soboo?*
Is there...	**Imate li…**	*eemate lee...*
- a safe?	**- sef?**	*- sef?*
- a babysitting service?	**- uslugu čuvanja djece?**	*- oosloogoo choovanya diyetse?*
- a laundry service?	**- uslugu pranja odjeće?**	*- oosloogoo pranya odyeche?*
Is there wheelchair access?	**Imate li pristup za invalidska kolica?**	*eemate lee preestoop za eenvaleedska koleetsa?*

Checking in & out

I have a reservation for tonight	**Imam rezervaciju za večeras**	*eemam rezervat-seeyoo za vercheras*
In the name of...	**Na ime...**	*na eeme...*
Here's my passport	**Izvolite moju putovnicu**	*eezvoleete moyoo pootovneetsoo*
What time is check out?	**Kada se moram odjaviti?**	*kada se moram odiyaveetee?*
Can I have a later check out?	**Mogu li se odjaviti kasnije?**	*mogoo lee se odiyaveetee kas-neeye?*
Can I leave my bags here?	**Mogu li ovdje ostaviti torbe?**	*mogoo lee ovdiye ostaveetee torbe?*
I'd like to check out	**Želim se odjaviti**	*zheleem se odiyaveetee*
Can I have the bill?	**Mogu li dobiti račun?**	*mogoo lee dobee-tee rachoon?*

Camping

Do you have...	**Imate li...**	*eemate lee...*
- a site available?	**- slobodno mjesto?**	*- slobodno miyesto?*
- electricity?	**- struju?**	*- strooyoo?*
- hot showers?	**- tuševe s toplom vodom?**	*- toosheve s toplom vodom?*
- tents for hire?	**- šatore za iznajmljivanje?**	*- shatore za eez-naymliyvanyea?*
How much is it per...	**Koliko naplaćujete po...**	*koleeko napla-chooyete po...*
- tent?	**- šatoru?**	*- shatoroo?*
- caravan?	**- kamp kućici?**	*- kamp koocheetsee?*
- person?	**- osobi?**	*- osobee?*
- car?	**- automobilu?**	*- aootomobeeloo?*
Where...	**Gdje...**	*gdiye...*
- is the reception?	**- je recepcija?**	*- ye retseptseeya?*
- are the bathrooms?	**- su kupaonice?**	*- soo koopaoneetse?*
- are the laundry facilities?	**- je praonica rublja?**	*- ye praoneetsa roobliya?*

Survival guide

Most people speak some English in touristy areas. Inland, however, German is more common, especially among the older generation. Avoid carrying Scottish pounds, which may be difficult to exchange.

This country is Catholic: don't try to visit a church in a swimming costume. Keep some loose change handy for public toilets. In parks, stay off the grass and sit on a bench instead. Above all, avoid discussing politics, wherever possible, which usually wastes time and creates animosity.

Money & banks

English	Croatian	Pronunciation
Where is the nearest...	**Gdje je...**	*gdyea ye...*
- bank?	**- najbliža banka?**	*- naiybleezha banka?*
- ATM/bank machine?	**- najbliži bankomat?**	*- naiybleezhee bankomat?*
- foreign exchange office?	**- najbliža mjenjačnica?**	*- naiybleezha miyeny-achneetsa?*
I'd like to...	**Želim...**	*zheleem...*
- withdraw money	**- isplatu**	*- eesplatoo*
- cash a traveller's cheque	**- unovčiti putnički ček**	*- oonovcheetee poo-tneechkee chek*
- change money	**- razmijeniti novac**	*- razmeeyeneetee novats*
- arrange a transfer	**- napraviti transfer**	*- napraveetee transfer*
Could I have smaller notes, please?	**Molim Vas isplatu u manjim novčanicama**	*moleem vas eespla-too oo manyeem novchaneetsama*
What's the exchange rate?	**Koji je kurs?**	*koyee ye koors?*
What's the commission?	**Kolika je provizija?**	*koleeka ye proveezeeya?*
What's the charge for...	**Koliko naplaćujete...**	*koleeko napla-chooyete...*
- making a withdrawal?	**- isplatu novca?**	*- isplatoo novtsa?*
- exchanging money?	**- razmjenu valute?**	*- razmiyenoo val-oote?*
- cashing a cheque?	**- mijenjanje čeka?**	*- meeyenyanye cheka?`*
What's the minimum/ maximum amount?	**Koji je najmanji/ najviši iznos?**	*koyee ye naiymany-ee/naiyveeshee eeznos?*
This is not right	**Ovo nije u redu**	*ovo neeye oo redoo*
Is there a problem with my account?	**Postoji li problem s računom?**	*postoyee lee problem s rachoonom?*
The ATM/bank machine took my card	**Bankomat mi je uzeo karticu**	*bankomat mee ye oozeo karteetsoo*
I've forgotten my PIN	**Zaboravio/Zaboravila** *m/f* **sam svoju lozinku**	*zaboraveeo/ zaboraveela sam svoyoo lozeenkoo*

Post office

Where is the (main) post office?	**Gdje je (glavna) pošta?**	*gdyea ye (glavna) poshta?*
I'd like to send a...	**Želim poslati…**	*zheleem poslatee...*
- letter	**- pismo**	*- peesmo*
- postcard	**- razglednicu**	*- razgledneetsoo*
- parcel	**- paket**	*- paket*
- fax	**- faks**	*- faks*
I'd like to send this...	**Želim ovo poslati…**	*zheleem ovo poslatee...*
- to the United Kingdom	**- u Veliku Britaniju**	*- oo veleekoo breetaneeyoo*
- by airmail	**- zračnom poštom**	*- zrachnom postom*
- by express mail	**- hitno**	*- heetno*
- by registered mail	**- preporučeno**	*- preporoocheno*
I'd like...	**Želim…**	*zheleem...*
- a stamp for this letter/postcard	**- marku za pismo/ razglednicu**	*- markoo za peesmo/ razgledneetsoo*
- to buy envelopes	**- kupiti omotnice**	*- koopeetee omotneetse*
- to make a photocopy	**- izraditi presliku**	*- eezradeetee presleekoo*
It's fragile	**Lako je lomljivo**	*lako ye lomlyeevo*

Don't roam

Buy a **Start paket** (*start paket*) with a local pre-pay SIM card from the Post Office, or VIP and T-mobile shops. The bundle usually includes about £10 worth of calls. Ask for English settings.

Telecoms

Where can I make an international phone call?	**Gdje mogu obaviti međunarodni poziv?**	*gdyea mogoo obaveetee mejoonarodnee pozeev?*

Where can I buy a phone card?	**Gdje mogu kupiti telefonsku karticu?**	*gdyea mogoo koopeetee telefonskoo karteetsoo?*
How do I call abroad?	**Kako se bira međunarodni broj?**	*kako se beera mejoonarodnee broy?*
How much does it cost per minute?	**Koliko košta minuta?**	*koleeko koshta meenoota?*
The number is...	**Broj je…**	*broy ye...*
What's the area/country code for...?	**Koji je pozivni broj za…?**	*koyee ye pozeevnee broy za...?*
The number is engaged	**Linija je zauzeta**	*leeneeya ye zaoozeta*
The connection is bad	**Veza je loša**	*veza ye losha*
I've been cut off	**Prekinula se linija**	*prekeenoola se leeneeya*
I'd like...	**Molim Vas…**	*moleem vas...*
- a charger for my mobile phone	**- punjač za moj mobitel**	*- poonyach za moy mobeetel*
- an adaptor plug	**- adapter za utičnicu**	*- adapter za ooteechneetsoo*
- a pre-paid SIM card	**- SIM karticu za doplatu bonovima**	*- seem kartitsoo za doplatoo bonoveema*

Internet

Where's the nearest Internet café?	**Gdje je najbliži internet café?**	*gdyea je naiybleezhee eenternet café?*
Can I access the Internet here?	**Mogu li se ovdje priključiti na internet?**	*mogoo lee se ovdiye preeklyoocheetee na eenternet?*
I'd like to...	**Želim…**	*zheleem...*
- use the Internet	**- koristiti internet**	*- koreesteetee eenternet*
- check my email	**- provjeriti mail**	*- proviyereetee mail*
- use a printer	**- koristiti pisač**	*- koreesteetee peesach*
How much is it...	**Koliko je…**	*koleeko ye...*

- per minute?	**- minuta?**	*- meenoota?*
- per hour?	**- sat?**	*- sat?*
- to buy a CD?	**- CD?**	*- tse de?*
How do I...	**Kako se…**	*kako se...*
- log on?	**- priključuje?**	*- preeklyoochooye?*
- open a browser?	**- otvara pretraživač?**	*- otvara preterazheevach?*
- print this?	**- radi ispis?**	*- radee eespees?*
I need help with this computer	**Treba mi pomoć s kompjutorom**	*treba mee pomoch s kompiyootorom*
The computer has crashed	**Kompjutor je pao**	*kompiyootor ye pao*
I've finished	**Gotov/a sam** *m/f*	*gotov/a sam*

Want to stay connected?
Not every hotel offers web access, so check large hotels and ACI marinas for Internet hotspots. If you are out in the sticks, just find something better to do!

Chemist

Where's the nearest (all-night) pharmacy?	**Gdje je najbliža (non-stop) ljekarna?**	*gdyea ye naiybleezha (non stop) lyekarna?*
What time does the pharmacy open/close?	**Kada se otvara/ zatvara ljekarna?**	*kada se otvara/zatvara lyekarna?*
I need something for...	**Treba mi nešto protiv…**	*treba mee nesto proteev...*
- diarrhoea	**- proljeva**	*- prolyeva*
- a cold	**- prehlade**	*- prehlade*

- a cough	**- kašlja**	*- kashlya*
- insect bites	**- uboda insekata**	*- ooboda eensekata*
- sunburn	**- opekotina od sunca**	*- opekoteena od soontsa*
- motion sickness	**- mučnine u vožnji**	*- moochneene oo vozhnyee*
- hay fever	**- peludne groznice**	*- peloodne grozneetse*
- period pain	**- menstrualnih bolova**	*- menstrooalneeh bolova*
- abdominal pains	**- bolova u trbuhu**	*- bolova oo ter-boohoo*
- a urine infection	**- urinarne infekcije**	*- ooreenarne eenfek-tseeye*
- a vaginal infection	**- vaginalne infekcije**	*- vageenalne eenfek-tseeye*
I'd like...	**Molim Vas…**	*moleem vas...*
- aspirin	**- aspirin**	*- aspeereen*
- plasters	**- flastere**	*- flastere*
- condoms	**- kondome**	*- kondome*
- insect repellent	**- nešto protiv komaraca**	*- neshto proteev komaratsa*
- painkillers	**- tablete protiv bolova**	*- tablete proteev bolova*
- a contraceptive	**- kontracepcijsko sredstvo**	*- kontratseptseeysko sredstvo*
How much should I take?	**Koju dozu trebam uzimati?**	*koyoo dozoo trebam oozeematee?*

24-hour city

Zagreb has a 24-hour pharmacy at Ilica 43 and a post office with currency exchange just outside the train station **Glavni kolodvor** (*glavnee kolodvor*). News kiosks can provide other essentials after hours.

Take...	**Uzimajte…**	*oozimaiytee...*
- a tablet	**- po jednu tabletu**	*- po yednoo tabletoo*
- a teaspoon	**- po jednu žličicu**	*- po yednoo zhleecheetsoo*
- with water	**- s vodom**	*- s vodom*
How often should I take this?	**Koliko puta dnevno?**	*koleeko poota dnevno?*
- once/twice a day	**- jedanput/dvaput na dan**	*- yedanpoot/dvapoot na dan*
- before/after meals	**- prije/poslije obroka**	*- preeye/posleeye obroka*
- in the morning/ evening	**- ujutro/uvečer**	*- ooyootro/oovecher*
Is it suitable for children?	**Može li se davati djeci?**	*mozhe lee se davatee diyetsee?*
Will it make me drowsy?	**Hoću li biti pospan/a** *m/f*?	*hochoo lee beetee pospan/a?*
Do I need a prescription?	**Treba li mi recept?**	*treba lee mee retsept?*
I have a prescription	**Imam recept**	*eemam retsept*

Children

Where should I take the children?	**Gdje mogu odvesti djecu?**	*gdyea mogoo odvestee diyetsoo?*
Where is the nearest...	**Gdje je najbliži…**	*gdyea ye naiybleezhee...*
- playground?	**- park s igralištem?**	*- park s eegraleestem?*
- fairground?	**- luna park?**	*- loona park*
- zoo?	**- zoološki vrt?**	*- zoloshkee vert?*
- swimming pool?	**- bazen?**	*- bazen?*
- park?	**- park?**	*- park?*
Is this suitable for children?	**Je li to prilagođeno za djecu?**	*ye lee to preelagojeno za diyetsoo?*
Are children allowed?	**Je li djeci dozvoljen pristup?**	*ye lee diyetsee dozvolyen preestoop?*
Are there baby-changing facilities here?	**Mogu li ovdje presvući bebu?**	*mogoo lee ovdiye presvoochee beboo?*

Do you have...	**Imate li…**	*eemate lee...*
- a children's menu?	**- dječji jelovnik?**	*- diyechiyee yelovneek?*
- a high chair?	**- dječji stolac?**	*- diyechiyee stolats?*
Is there...	**Postoji li ovdje…**	*postoyee lee ovdiye...*
- a child-minding service?	**- čuvanje djece?**	*- choovaniye diyetse?*
- a nursery?	**- dječji vrtić?**	*- diyechiyee ver-teech?*
Can you recommend a reliable babysitter?	**Možete li mi preporučiti dobru čuvateljicu?**	*mozhete lee mee preporoocheetee dobroo choovatelyeetsoo?*
Are the children constantly supervised?	**Jesu li djeca pod stalnim nadzorom?**	*yesoo lee diyetsa pod stalneem nad-sorom?*
When can I bring them?	**Kada ih mogu dovesti?**	*kada ih mogoo dovestee?*
What time do I have to pick them up?	**Kada moram doći po njih?**	*kada moram dochee po nyeeh?*
He/she is... years old	**On/ona ima… godina**	*on/ona eema... godeena*
I'd like to buy...	**Želim kupiti…**	*zheleem koopeetee...*
- nappies	**- pelene**	*- pelene*
- baby wipes	**- vlažne dječje maramice**	*- vlazhne diyechiye marameetse*
- tissues	**- maramice**	*- marameetse*

Travellers with disabilities

I have a disability	**Ja sam invalid**	*ya sam eenvaleed*
I need assistance	**Treba mi pomoć**	*treba mee pomoch*
I am blind	**Ja sam slijep/a** *m/f*	*ya sam sleeyep/a*
I am deaf	**Ja sam gluh/a** *m/f*	*ya sam glooh/a*
I have a hearing aid	**Nosim slušni aparat**	*noseem slooshnee aparat*
I can't walk well	**Teško hodam**	*teshko hodam*
Is there a lift?	**Postoji li dizalo?**	*postoyee lee deezalo?*
Is there wheelchair access?	**Postoji li pristup za invalidska kolica?**	*postoyee lee preestoop za een-valeedska koleetsa?*

Can I bring my guide dog?	**Mogu li dovesti psa vodiča?**	*mogoo lee dovestee psa vodeecha?*
Are there disabled toilets?	**Postoji li WC za invalide?**	*postoyee lee vey tsey za een-valeede?*
Do you offer disabled services?	**Nudite li usluge za invalide?**	*noodeete lee ooslooge za eenvaleede?*
Could you help me...	**Možete li mi pomoći…**	*mozhete lee mee pomochee...*
- cross the street?	**- preko ceste?**	*- preko tseste?*
- go up the stairs?	**- po stepenicama?**	*- po stepeneetsama?*
- go down the stairs?	**- niz stepenice?**	*- neez stepeneetse?*
Can I sit down somewhere?	**Mogu li negdje sjesti?**	*mogoo lee negdiyea siyestee?*
Could you call a disabled taxi for me?	**Možete li mi pozvati taksi za invalide?**	*mozhete lee mee pozvatee taksee za eenvaleede?*

Repairs & cleaning

This is broken	**Pokvarilo se**	*pokvareelo se*
Can you fix it?	**Možete li popraviti?**	*mozhete lee popraveetee?*
Do you have...	**Imate li…**	*eemate lee...*
- a battery?	**- akumulator?**	*- akoomoolator?*
- spare parts?	**- rezervne dijelove?**	*- rezervne deeyelove?*
Can you... this?	**Možete li ovo…**	*mozhete lee ovo...*
- clean	**- očistiti?**	*- ocheesteetee?*
- press	**- ispeglati?**	*- eespeglatee?*
- dry-clean	**- kemijski očistiti?**	*- kemeeyskee ocheesteetee?*
- patch	**- zakrpati?**	*- zakerpatee?*
When will it be ready?	**Kada će biti gotovo?**	*kada che beetee gotovo?*
This isn't mine	**Ovo nije moje**	*ovo neeye moye*

Tourist information

Where's the Tourist Information Office?	**Gdje je turistički ured?**	*gdiyea ye tooreesteechkee oored?*

Do you have a city/regional map?	**Imate li plan grada/regionalnu kartu?**	*eemate lee plan grada/regeeonal-noo kartoo?*
What are the main places of interest?	**Gdje su glavne zanimljivosti?**	*gdiyea soo glavne zaneemlyeevostee?*
Could you show me on the map?	**Molim Vas pokažite mi na karti**	*moleem vas pokazheetee mee na kartee?*
We'll be here for...	**Ostajemo…**	*ostaiyemo...*
- half a day	**- pola dana**	*- pola dana*
- a day	**- jedan dan**	*- yedan dan*
- a week	**- tjedan dana**	*- tiyedan dana*
Do you have a brochure in English?	**Imate li prospekt na engleskom?**	*eemate lee prospekt na engleskom?*
We're interested in...	**Zanima nas…**	*zaneema nas...*
- history	**- povijest**	*- poveeyest*
- architecture	**- arhitektura**	*- arheetektoora*
- shopping	**- kupovina**	*- koopoveena*
- hiking	**- pješačenje u prirodi**	*- piyeshacheniye oo preerodee*
- a scenic walk	**- panoramska šetnja**	*- panoramska shet-nya*
- a boat cruise	**- izlet brodom**	*- eezlet brodom*
- a guided tour	**- obilazak s vodičem**	*- obeelazak s vodeechem*
Are there any excursions?	**Nudite li kakve izlete?**	*noodeetee lee kakve eezlete?*
How long does it take?	**Koliko dugo traje?**	*koleeko doogo traiye?*
What does it cost?	**Koliko košta?**	*koleeko koshta?*

Emergencies

Reciprocal health agreements mean that British citizens can receive free emergency treatment in Croatia. Other medical services require immediate cash payment. For mild complaints, ask a pharmacist for advice.

Always keep your passport with you, in a safe place. Croatian law requires ID papers to be carried at all times. When abroad, it is always good to have your embassy's details. For this and other handy information, check out www.britishembassy.gov.uk/croatia and make a note of useful numbers and names, such as English-speaking lawyers.

Medical

Where is...	**Gdje je…**	*gdye ye...*
- the hospital?	**- bolnica?**	*- bolneetsa?*
- the health centre?	**- zdravstveni centar?**	*- zdravstvenee tsentar?*
I need...	**Treba mi…**	*treba mee...*
- a doctor	**- doktor**	*- doktor*
- a female doctor	**- doktorica**	*- doktoreetsa*
- an ambulance	**- hitna pomoć**	*- heetna pomoch*
It's very urgent	**Vrlo je hitno**	*verlo ye heetno*
I'm injured	**Ozlijeđen/a** *m/f* **sam**	*ozleeyejen/a sam*
Can I see the doctor?	**Mogu li vidjeti doktora?**	*mogoo lee veedyetee doktora?*
I don't feel well	**Ne osjećam se dobro**	*ne osyecham se dobro*
I have...	**Imam…**	*eemam...*
- a cold	**- prehladu**	*- prehladoo*
- diarrhoea	**- proljev**	*- proliyev*
- a rash	**- osip**	*- osip*
- a temperature	**- temperaturu**	*- temperatooroo*
I have a lump here	**Ovdje imam kvržicu**	*ovdiye eemam kverzheetsoo*
Can I have the morning-after pill?	**Mogu li dobiti pilulu za jutro poslije?**	*mogoo lee dobeetee peelooloo za yootro posliyea?*
It hurts here	**Ovdje me boli**	*ovdiye me bolee*
It hurts a lot/a little	**Jako/malo me boli**	*yako/malo me bolee*
How much do I owe you?	**Koliko Vam dugujem?**	*koleeko vam doo-gooyem?*
I have insurance	**Imam osiguranje**	*eemam osee-gooranyea*

Dentist

I need a dentist	**Trebam zubara**	*trebam zoobara*
I have tooth ache	**Boli me zub**	*bolee me zoob*
My gums are swollen	**Natečene su mi desni**	*natechene soo mee desnee*
This filling has fallen out	**Ispala mi je plomba**	*eespala mee ye plomba*

I have an abscess	**Imam apsces**	*eemam apstses*
I've broken a tooth	**Slomio mi se zub**	*slomeeo mee se zoob*
Are you going to take it out?	**Hoćete li vaditi?**	*hochete lee vadee-tee?*
Can you fix it temporarily?	**Možete li to privremeno popraviti?**	*mozhete lee to preevremeno popraveetee?*

Crime

I want to report a theft	**Želim prijaviti krađu**	*zheleem preeyavee-tee krajoo*
Someone has stolen my...	**Netko mi je ukrao...**	*netko mee ye ookrao...*
- bag	**- torbu**	*- torboo*
- car	**- auto**	*- aooto*
- credit cards	**- kreditne kartice**	*- kredeetne kar-teetse*
- money	**- novac**	*- novats*
- passport	**- putovnicu**	*- pootovneetsoo*
I've been attacked	**Netko me je napao**	*netko me ye napao*

Emergencies 112

Call this general number in case of an emergency. It provides access to police, ambulance and fire brigade services, as well as the mountain rescue.

Lost property

I've lost my...	**Izgubio/Izgubila** *m/f* **sam...**	*eezgoobio/eezgoobi-la sam...*
- car keys	**- ključeve od auta**	*- kliyoocheve od aoota*
- driving licence	**- vozačku dozvolu**	*- vozachkoo dozvoloo*

- handbag	**- ručnu torbu**	*- roochnoo torboo*
- flight tickets	**- avionske karte**	*- aveeonske karte*
It happened...	**To se dogodilo...**	*to se dogodeelo...*
- this morning	**- danas ujutro**	*- danas ooyootro*
- today	**- danas**	*- danas*
- in the hotel	**- u hotelu**	*- oo hoteloo*
I left it in the taxi	**Ostalo je u taksiju**	*ostalo ye oo takseeyoo*

Breakdowns

I've had...	**Imao/Imala** *m/f* **sam...**	*eemao/eemala sam...*
- an accident	**- sudar**	*- soodar*
- a breakdown	**- kvar**	*- kvar*
- a puncture	**- puknutu gumu**	*- pooknootoo goomoo*
My battery is flat	**Prazan mi je akumulator**	*prazan mee ye akoomoolator*
I don't have a spare tyre	**Nemam rezervnu gumu**	*nemam rezervnoo goomoo*
I've run out of petrol	**Nestalo mi je benzina**	*nestalo mee ye benzeena*
My car doesn't start	**Ne pali mi auto**	*ne palee mee aooto*
Can you repair it?	**Možete li popraviti?**	*mozhete lee popraveetee?*
How long will you be?	**Koliko će to trajati?**	*koleeko che to trai-yatee?*
I have breakdown cover	**Imam osiguranje za slučaj kvara na autu**	*eemam oseegooranye za sloochaye kvara na aootoo*

Problems with the authorities

I'm sorry, I didn't realise...	**Žao mi je ali nisam shvatio/shvatila** *(m/f)*...	*zhao mee ye alee neesam shvateeo/ shvateela...*
- I was driving so fast	**- da vozim tako brzo**	*- da vozeem tako berzo*
- I went over the red lights	**- da prolazim kroz crveno**	*- da prolazeem kroz tserveno*
- it was against the law	**- da je to protuzakonito**	*- da ye to protoozakoneeto*
Here are my documents	**Izvolite moje dokumente**	*eezvoleete moye dokoomente*
I'm innocent	**Nevin/Nevina** *m/f* **sam**	*neveen/neveena sam*

Dictionary

Construct your own sentences using our English-Croatian dictionary, and use the Croatian-English version to work out the responses. Nouns are nominative, verbs infinitive and adjectives neutral. To turn them into feminine or masculine form, here's a tip – feminine words most commonly end with "a", neutral with "o" and masculine with a consonant: **lijepa planina** (beautiful mountain), **lijepo nebo** (beautiful sky), **lijep potok** (beautiful spring). Adjectives come before nouns and agree with nouns in gender. Don't worry too much about making mistakes, though: Croats will be thrilled you've made even a minimal effort to speak their lingo.

English-Croatian dictionary

A		
a (n)	**jedan**	*yedan*
about (concerning)	**o**	*o*
accident	**nezgoda**	*nezgoda*
accident (car)	**sudar**	*soodar*
accommodation	**smještaj**	*smyeshtiye*
A&E	**hitna pomoć**	*heetna pomoch*
aeroplane	**zrakoplov**	*zrakoplov*
again	**ponovo**	*ponovo*
ago	**prije**	*preeye*
AIDS	**SIDA**	*seeda*
airmail	**zračna pošta**	*zrachna poshta*
airport	**zračna luka**	*zrachna looka*
alarm	**uzbuna**	*oozboona*
all	**sve**	*sve*
all right	**u redu**	*oo redoo*
allergy	**alergija**	*alergiya*
ambulance	**kola hitne pomoći**	*kola heetne pomochi*
America	**Amerika**	*amerika*
American	**američki**	*amereechkee*
and	**i**	*ee*
anniversary	**godišnjica**	*godishnyitsa*
another	**drugo**	*droogo*
to answer	**odgovoriti**	*odgovoreetee*
any	**bilo koje**	*beelo koyee*
apartment	**apartman**	*apartman*
appointment	**(zakazani) sastanak**	*(zakazanee) sastanak*
April	**travanj**	*travanye*
area	**područje**	*podroochyea*
area code	**pozivni broj**	*pozeevnee broy*
around	**oko**	*oko*
to arrange	**dogovoriti**	*dogovoreetee*
arrival	**dolazak**	*dolazak*
art	**umjetnost**	*oomyetnost*
to ask	**pitati**	*peetatee*
aspirin	**aspirin**	*aspeereen*
at (place)	**kod**	*kod*
at (time)	**u**	*oo*
August	**kolovoz**	*kolovoz*
Australia	**Australija**	*aoostraleeya*
Australian	**australski**	*aoostralskee*
available	**slobodno**	*slobodno*
away	**odsutno**	*odsootno*
B		
baby	**beba**	*beba*
back (place)	**iza**	*eeza*
baggage	**prtljaga**	*prtlyaga*
bar (pub)	**bar**	*bar*
bath (room)	**kupaonica**	*koopaonitsa*
bath (tub)	**kada**	*kada*
bathing cap	**kapa za tuširanje**	*kapa za tooshiranyea*

to be	**biti**	*beetee*

beach **plaža** ***plazha***
Sandy stretches are rare, but the large rocks are ideal for swimming from into the sea.

because	**jer**	*yer*
best	**najbolje**	*nayebolye*
better	**bolje**	*bolye*
between	**između**	*eezmejoo*
bicycle	**bicikl**	*beeceekl*
big	**veliko**	*veleeko*
bill	**račun**	*rachoon*
bit (a)	**malo**	*malo*
boarding card	**ukrcajna karta**	*ookrtsayena karta*
book	**knjiga**	*knyeega*
to book	**rezervirati**	*rezerveeratee*
booking	**rezervacija**	*rezervatseeya*
box office	**blagajna**	*blagayna*
boy	**dječak**	*dyechak*
brother	**brat**	*brat*
bullfight	**korida**	*koreeda*
bureau de change	**mjenjačnica**	*myenyachnitsa*
to burn	**zapaliti**	*zapaleetee*
bus	**autobus**	*aootoboos*
business	**posao**	*posao*
business class	**poslovni razred**	*poslovnee razred*
but	**ali**	*alee*
to buy	**kupiti**	*koopitee*
by (beside)	**pokraj**	*pokraye*
by (via)	**preko**	*preko*

C

café	**kafić, kavana**	*kafeech, kavana*
calculator	**kalkulator, digitron**	*kalkoolator, deegeetron*
to call	**zvati**	*zvatee*
camera	**foto aparat**	*foto aparat*
can (to be able)	**moći**	*mochee*
to cancel	**otkazati**	*otkazatee*
car	**automobil**	*aootomobeel*
carton (cigarettes)	**šteka**	*shteka*
cash	**gotovina**	*gotoveena*
cash point	**bankomat**	*bankomat*
casino	**kasino**	*kaseeno*

cathedral **katedrala** ***katedrala***
Zagreb's cathedral was first built in 1217 then restored to neo-gothic postcard perfection in 1906.

CD	**cd**	*tse de*
centre	**centar**	*tsentar*
to change	**promijeniti**	*promeeyeneetee*
charge	**naplata**	*naplata*
to charge	**naplatiti**	*naplateetee*
cheap	**jeftino**	*yefteeno*

to check in	**prijaviti**	*preeaveetee*
cheque	**ček**	*chek*
child	**dijete**	*diyete*
cigar	**cigara**	*tseegara*
cigarette	**cigareta**	*tseegareta*
cinema	**kino**	*keeno*
city	**grad**	*grad*
to close	**zatvoriti**	*zatvoreetee*
close by	**blizu**	*bleezoo*
closed	**zatvoreno**	*zatvoreno*
clothes	**odjeća**	*odyecha*
club	**klub**	*kloob*
coast	**obala**	*obala*
cold	**hladno**	*hladno*
colour	**boja**	*boya*
to complain	**žaliti se**	*zhaleetee se*
complaint	**žalba**	*zhalba*
to confirm	**potvrditi**	*potvrdeetee*
confirmation	**potvrda**	*potvrda*
congratulations!	**čestitam!**	*chesteetam!*
consulate	**konzulat**	*konzoolat*
to contact	**kontaktirati**	*kontakteeratee*
contagious	**zarazno**	*zarazno*
cool	**hladno**	*hladno*
cost	**cijena**	*tsyena*
to cost	**koštati**	*kostatee*
cot	**dječji krevet**	*dyechyee krevet*
country	**država**	*drzhava*
countryside	**priroda**	*preeroda*
cream	**vrhnje**	*vrhnye*
credit card	**kreditna kartica**	*kredeetna karteetsa*
crime	**kriminal**	*kreemeenal*
Croatia	**Hrvatska**	*hervatska*
Croatian	**hrvatski**	*hervatski*

currency **valuta** ***valoota***
The Croatian national currency is the kuna (HK or Kn), but many establishments accept euros too.

customer	**stranka**	*stranka*
customs	**carina**	*tsareena*
cut	**posjekotina**	*posyekoteena*
to cut	**rezati**	*rezatee*
cycling	**vožnja biciklom**	*vozhnya beetseeklom*

D

damage	**šteta**	*shteta*
date (calendar)	**datum**	*datoom*
daughter	**kćer**	*kcher*
day	**dan**	*dan*
December	**prosinac**	*proseenats*
to dehydrate	**dehidrirati**	*deheedreeratee*
delay	**(za)kašnjenje**	*(za)kashnyenye*
to dial (a number)	**birati (broj)**	*beeratee (broy)*
difficult	**teško**	*teshko*

dining room	blagovaonica	*blagovaonitsa*
directions	upute	*oopoote*
dirty	prljavo	*prlyavo*
disable	onesposobiti	*onesposobeetee*
disco	disko	*deesko*
discount	popust	*popoost*
disinfectant	dezinfekcijsko sredstvo	*dezeenfektseeysko sredstvo*
to disturb	smetati	*smetatee*
doctor	doktor	*doktor*
double	duplo	*dooplo*
down	dolje	*dolye*
to drive	voziti	*vozeetee*
driver	vozač	*vozach*

driving licence vozačka dozvola ***vozachka dozvola***
Drivers must carry their licence, proof of insurance and vehicle registration papers in the car.

drug	droga	*droga*
to dry clean	kemijsko čišćenje	*kemeeysko tseeshchenye*
dry-cleaner's	kemijska čistionica	*kemeeyska cheesteeonitsa*
during	tijekom	*teeyekom*
duty (tax)	porez	*porez*

E

early	rano	*rano*
to eat	jesti	*yestee*
electricity	struja	*strooya*
e-mail	e-mail	*ee-mail*
embassy	veleposlanstvo	*veleposlanstvo*
emergency	hitni slučaj	*heetnee sloochaye*
England	Engleska	*engleska*
English	engleski	*engleskee*
to enjoy	uživati	*oozheevati*
enough	dosta	*dosta*
error	pogreška	*pogreshka*
exactly	točno	*tochno*
exchange rate	kurs	*koors*
exhibition	Izložba	*eezlozhba*
to export	izvoziti	*eezvozeetee*
express (delivery)	hitno	*heetno*
express (train)	ekspresni vlak	*ekspresnee vlak*

F

facilities	pogodnosti	*pogodnostee*
far	daleko	*daleko*
fast	brzo	*brzo*
father	otac	*otats*
favourite	omiljeno	*omeelyeno*
to fax	faksirati	*fakseeratee*
February	veljača	*velyacha*
filling (station)	benzinska postaja	*benzeenska postaya*

film (camera)	**film**	*feelm*
film (cinema)	**film**	*feelm*

Medieval Motovun in Istria forms a dramatic backdrop for the highly esteemed Motovun Film Festival.

to finish	**završiti**	*zavursheetee*
fire	**vatra**	*vatra*
first aid	**prva pomoć**	*prva pomoch*
fitting room	**kabina**	*kabeena*
flight	**let**	*let*
flu	**gripa**	*greepa*
food poisoning	**trovanje hranom**	*trovanye hranom*
football	**nogomet**	*nogomet*
for	**za**	*za*
form (document)	**obrazac**	*obrazats*
free (money)	**besplatno**	*besplatno*
free (vacant)	**slobodno**	*slobodno*
friend	**prijatelj**	*preeyatelye*
from	**od**	*od*

G

gallery	**galerija**	*galereeya*
garage	**garaža**	*garazha*
gas	**plin**	*pleen*
gents	**muški WC**	*mooshkee ve tse*
to get	**dobiti**	*dobeetee*
girl	**djevojčica, djevojka**	*dyevoycheetsa, dyevoyka*
to give	**dati**	*dati*
glasses	**naočale**	*naochale*
to go	**ići**	*eechee*
golf	**golf**	*golf*
golf course	**golf igralište**	*golf eegralishte*
good	**dobro**	*dobro*
group	**grupa**	*groopa*
guarantee	**garancija**	*garantsiya*
guide	**vodič**	*vodich*

H

hair	**kosa**	*kosa*
hairdresser's	**frizer**	*frizer*
half	**pola**	*pola*
to have	**imati**	*eematee*
heat	**vrućina**	*vroocheena*
help!	**upomoć!**	*oopomoch!*
to help	**pomoći**	*pomochee*
here	**ovdje**	*ovdyea*
high	**visoko**	*veesoko*
to hire	**unajmiti**	*oonayemeetee*
holiday	**odmor**	*odmor*
holidays	**praznici**	*praznitsee*
homosexual	**homoseksualno**	*homoseksooalno*
horse riding	**jahanje**	*yahanye*
hospital	**bolnica**	*bolneetsa*

hot	vruće	*vrooche*
how?	kako?	*kako?*
how big?	koliko veliko?	*koleeko veleeko?*
how far?	koliko daleko?	*koleeko daleko?*
how long?	koliko dugo?	*koleeko doogo?*
how much?	koliko?	*koleeko?*
to be hungry	gladovati	*gladovatee*
hurry up!	požuri!	*pozhooree*
to hurt	boliti	*boleetee*
husband	suprug	*sooproog*

I

identity card	osobna iskaznica	*osobna eeskazneetsa*
ill	bolesno	*bolesno*
immediately	smjesta	*smyesta*
to import	uvesti	*oovestee*
important	važno	*vazhno*
in	u	*oo*
information	informacija	*informatsiya*
inside	unutra	*oonootra*
insurance	osiguranje	*osigooranje*
interesting	zanimljivo	*zaneemlyeevo*

international međunarodno *mejoonarodno*
International events include Eurokaz (modern theatre), Pula Film Festival and the magnificent Dubrovnik Summer Festival.

Ireland	Irska	*eerska*
Irish	irski	*eerski*
island	otok	*otok*
itinerary	plan puta	*plan poota*

J

January	siječanj	*seeyechanye*

jellyfish meduza *medooza*
Swarms of Jellyfish can sometimes make the shore unappealing. Follow locals' advice and go sightseeing instead.

jet ski	vodeni skuter	*vodeni skooter*
journey	putovanje	*pootovanyea*
July	srpanj	*serpanye*
junction	raskrižje	*razkrizhye*
June	lipanj	*leepanye*
just (only)	samo	*samo*

K

to keep	(za)držati	*(za)derzhatee*
key	ključ	*klyooch*
key ring	privjesak za ključeve	*preevyesak za klyoo-cheve*
keyboard	klavijatura	*klaveeyatoora*
kid	klinac/klinka	*kleenats/kleenka*

to kill	**ubiti**	*oobeetee*
kind (nice)	**drago, prijazno**	*drago, preeyasno*
kind (sort)	**vrsta**	*versta*
kiosk	**kiosk**	*keeosk*
kiss	**poljubac**	*polyoobats*
to kiss	**ljubiti**	*lyoobeetee*
to knock	**kucati**	*kootsatee*
to know (knowledge)	**znati**	*znatee*
to know (person)	**poznavati**	*poznavatee*

L

label	**etiketa, marka**	*eteeketa, marka*
ladies (toilets)	**ženski wc**	*zhenskee ve tse*
lady	**dama**	*dama*
language	**jezik**	*yezeek*
last	**posljednje**	*poslyednyea*
late (delayed)	**zakašnjelo**	*zakashnyelo*
late (time)	**kasno**	*kasno*
launderette	**praonica veša**	*praoneetsa vesha*
lawyer	**odvjetnik**	*odvyetneek*
to leave	**ostaviti, otići**	*ostaveetee, oteechee*
left	**otišlo**	*oteeshlo*
less	**manje**	*manyea*
letter	**pismo**	*peesmo*
library	**knjižnica**	*knyeezhneetsa*
life jacket	**prsluk za spašavanje**	*perslook za spashavanyea*
lifeguard	**spasilac**	*spasilats*
lift	**dizalo**	*deezalo*

to like — **sviđati se** — ***sveejatee se***
Kids are welcome almost everywhere and are commonly given sweets by well-intentioned strangers.

to listen to	**slušati**	*slooshatee*
little (a little)	**malo**	*malo*
local	**lokalno**	*lokalno*
to look	**gledati**	*gledatee*
to lose	**izgubiti**	*izgoobeetee*
lost and found property (office)	**(ured za) izgubljeno-nađeno**	*(oored za) eez-gooblyeno-najeno*
luggage	**prtljaga**	*pertlyaga*

M

madam	**gospođa**	*gospoja*
mail	**pošta**	*poshta*
main	**glavni**	*glavnee*
to make	**napraviti**	*napraveetee*
man	**muškarac**	*mooshkarats*
manager	**menadžer**	*menadjer*
many	**mnogo**	*mnogo*
map (city)	**plan grada**	*plan grada*
map (road)	**karta**	*karta*
March	**ožujak**	*ozhooyak*
market	**tržnica**	*terzhneetsa*

married	**vjenčano**	*vyenchano*
May	**svibanj**	*sveebanye*
maybe	**možda**	*mozhda*
mechanic	**mehaničar**	*mehaneechar*
to meet	**susresti**	*soosrestee*
meeting	**sastanak**	*sastanak*
message	**poruka**	*porooka*
midday	**podne**	*podne*
midnight	**ponoć**	*ponoch*
minimum	**minimum**	*meeneemoom*
minute	**minuta**	*meenoota*
to miss (a person)	**nedostajati**	*nedostayatee*
to miss (a train)	**propustiti**	*propoosteetee*
missing	**nestalo**	*nestalo*
mobile phone	**mobilni telefon**	*mobeelni telefon*
moment	**trenutak**	*trenootak*
money	**novac**	*novats*
more	**više**	*veeshe*
mosquito	**komarac**	*komarats*
most	**naj, vrlo**	*naye, verlo*
mother	**majka**	*mayka*
much	**puno**	*poono*
museum	**muzej**	*moozey*
musical	**mjuzikl**	*myoozeekl*
must	**morati**	*moratee*
my	**moj**	*moy*

N

name	**ime**	*eeme*
nationality	**nacionalnost**	*natseeonalnost*
near	**blizu**	*bleezoo*
necessary	**neophodno**	*neophodno*
to need	**trebati**	*trebatee*
never	**nikad**	*neekad*
new	**novo**	*novo*

news | **vijesti** | ***veeyestee***
Hrvatski Radio II – 98.5 MHz – broadcasts news and traffic information in English during the tourist season.

newspaper	**novine**	*noveene*
next	**sljedeće**	*slyedeche*
next to	**do, pokraj**	*do, pokraye*
nice (people)	**ugodno, ljubazno**	*oogodno, lyoobazno*
nice (things)	**lijepo**	*leeyepo*
night	**noć**	*noch*
nightclub	**noćni klub**	*nochnee kloob*
north	**sjever**	*syever*
note (money)	**novčanica**	*novchaneetsa*
nothing	**ništa**	*neeshta*
November	**studeni**	*stoodenee*
now	**sad**	*sad*
nowhere	**nigdje**	*neegdyea*
nudist beach	**nudistička plaža**	*noodeesteechka plazha*
number	**broj**	*broy*

O

object	**objekt**	*obyekt*
October	**listopad**	*leestopad*
off (food)	**pokvareno**	*pokvareno*
off (switched)	**isključeno**	*eesklyoocheno*
office	**ured**	*oored*
OK	**ok**	*okay*
on	**na**	*na*
once	**jednom**	*yednom*
only	**samo, jedino**	*samo, yedeeno*
open	**otvoreno**	*otvoreno*
to open	**otvoriti**	*otvoreetee*
operator	**centrala**	*tsentrala*
opposite (place)	**preko puta**	*preko poota*
optician's	**optičar**	*opteechar*
or	**ili**	*eelee*
to order	**naručiti**	*naroocheetee*
other	**drugo**	*droogo*
out of order	**pokvareno**	*pokvareno*
outdoor	**na otvorenom**	*na otvorenom*
outside	**vani**	*vanee*
overnight	**preko noći**	*preko nochee*
owner	**vlasnik**	*vlasnik*
oxygen	**kisik**	*keeseek*

P

painkiller	**tableta protiv bolova**	*tableta proteev bolova*
pair	**par**	*par*
parents	**roditelji**	*rodeetelye*
park	**park**	*park*
to park	**parkirati**	*parkeeratee*
parking	**parkiralište**	*parkeeraleeshte*
party	**zabava**	*zabava*
passport	**putovnica**	*pootovnitsa*
to pay	**platiti**	*plateetee*
people	**ljudi**	*lyoodee*
perhaps	**možda**	*mozhda*
person	**osoba**	*osoba*
phone	**telefon**	*telefon*
to phone	**telefonirati**	*telefoneeratee*
photo	**fotografija**	*fotografeeya*
phrase book	**frazeološki rječnik**	*frazeoloshki riyechneek*
place	**mjesto**	*miyesto*
platform	**peron**	*peron*
police	**policija**	*poleetseeya*
port (drink)	**port**	*port*
port (sea)	**pristanište (luka)**	*preestaneeshte (looka)*
possible	**moguće**	*mogooche*

post (office) — **pošta** — ***poshta***
Additional services at the post office include currency exchange, pre-pay mobile phone top-up and fax machines.

to prefer	**davati prednost**	*davatee prednost*
prescription	**recept**	*retsept*

pretty	lijepo	*leeyepo*
price	cijena	*tseeyena*
private	privatno	*preevatno*
probably	vjerojatno	*viyeroyatno*
problem	problem	*problem*
pub	pab, bar	*pab, bar*
public transport	javni prijevoz	*yavnee preeyevoz*
to put	staviti	*staveetee*

Q

quality	**kvaliteta**	***kvaleeteta***

Some of Europe's best oysters come from Mali Ston bay, northwest of Dubrovnik.

quantity	kvantiteta	*kvanteeteta*
quarter	četvrt	*chetvert*
query	upit	*oopeet*
question	pitanje	*peetanyea*
queue	red	*red*
quick	brzo	*berzo*
quiet	tiho	*teeho*
quite	prilično	*preeleechno*
quiz	kviz	*kveez*

R

radio	radio	*radio*
railway	željeznica	*zhelyezneetsa*
rain	kiša	*keesha*
rape	silovanje	*seelovanye*
razor blade	žilet	*zheelet*
ready	gotovo	*gotovo*
real	stvarno	*stvarno*
receipt	račun	*rachoon*
to receive	primiti	*preemeetee*
reception	recepcija	*retseptsiya*
receptionist	recepcionar	*retseptseeonar*
to recommend	preporučiti	*preporoocheetee*
reduction	popust	*popoost*
to refund	vratiti (novac)	*vrateetee (novats)*
to refuse	odbiti	*odbeetee*
to relax	opustiti (se)	*opoosteetee (se)*
rent	stanarina	*stanareena*
to rent	unajmiti	*oonaiymeetee*
to request	zatražiti	*zatrazheetee*
reservation	rezervacija	*rezervatseeya*
to reserve	rezervirati	*rezerveeratee*
retired	umirovljenik	*oomirovliyeneek*
rich	bogato	*bogato*
to ride (horse)	jahati	*yahatee*
to ride (scooter)	voziti	*vozeetee*
right	desno	*desno*
to be right	biti u pravu	*beetee oo pravoo*
to ring (phone)	nazvati	*nazvatee*
to ring (bell)	pozvoniti	*pozvoneetee*

road	**cesta**	*tsesta*
to rob	**opljačkati**	*opliyachkatee*
room	**soba**	*soba*
route	**smjer puta**	*smyer poota*
rude	**Prosto**	*prosto*
ruins	**ruševine**	*roosheveene*
to run	**trčati**	*terchatee*

S

safe	**sigurno**	*sigoorno*
sauna	**sauna**	*saoona*
Scotland	**Škotska**	*shkotska*
Scottish	**škotski**	*shkotski*
sea	**more**	*more*
seat	**sjedalo**	*siyedalo*
seat belt	**pojas**	*poyas*
sedative	**sedativ**	*sedateev*
see you later	**vidimo se**	*veedeemo se*
self-service	**samoposluga**	*samoposlooga*
to sell	**prodati**	*prodatee*
to send	**poslati**	*poslatee*
sensible	**razumno**	*razoomno*

September **rujan** ***rooyan***
September is warm, gloriously colourful, and flavoured with roast corn, ripe grapes and wine.

to serve	**poslužiti**	*posloozheetee*
service	**usluga**	*ooslooga*
shop	**prodavaonica**	*prodavaoneetsa*
shopping	**kupovina**	*koopoveena*
shopping centre	**šoping centar**	*shoping tsentar*
short	**kratko**	*kratko*
show	**predstava**	*predstava*
to show	**pokazati**	*pokazatee*
shut	**zatvoreno**	*zatvoreno*
sign	**znak**	*znak*
to sign	**potpisati**	*potpeesatee*
signature	**potpis**	*potpees*
since	**od**	*od*
sir	**gospodin**	*gospodin*
sister	**sestra**	*sestra*
ski	**skijanje**	*skeeyanyea*
to sleep	**spavati**	*spavatee*
sleeping pill	**tableta za spavanje**	*tableta za spavanyea*
slow	**polagano**	*polagano*
small	**malo**	*malo*
to smoke	**pušiti**	*poosheetee*
soft	**mekano**	*mekano*
some	**nekoliko**	*nekoleeko*
something	**nešto**	*neshto*
son	**sin**	*seen*
soon	**uskoro**	*ooskoro*
south	**jug**	*yoog*
South Africa	**Južna Afrika**	*yoozhna afreeka*

South African	južnoafrički	*yoozhnoafreechkee*
speed	brzina	*berzeena*
to spell	spelovati	*spelovatee*
sport	sport	*sport*
stadium	stadion	*stadeeon*
staff	osoblje	*osoblyea*
stamp	marka	*marka*
to start	započeti	*zapochetee*
to start (car)	upaliti auto	*oopaleetee aooto*
station	stanica	*stanitsa*
sterling pound	funta sterlinga	*foonta sterleenga*
to stop	stati	*statee*
to stop (someone)	zaustaviti	*zaoostaveetee*
straight	ravno	*ravno*
street	ulica	*oolitsa*
stress	stres	*stres*
suddenly	iznenada	*eeznenada*
suitcase	kofer	*kofer*
sun	sunce	*soontse*
sunglasses	sunčane naočale	*soonchane naoochale*
surname	prezime	*prezeeme*
to swim	plivati	*pleevatee*
swimming pool	bazen	*bazen*
symptom	simptom	*seemptom*

T

table	stol	*stol*
to take	uzeti	*oozetee*
tall	visoko	*veesoko*
tampons	tamponi	*tamponee*
tax	porez	*porez*
tax free	bez poreza	*bez poreza*
taxi	taxi	*taksee*
taxi rank	taxi stajalište	*taksee staiyaleeshte*
telephone	telefon	*telefon*
telephone box	telefonska govornica	*telefonska govorneetsa*
television	televizija	*televeezeeya*
tennis	tenis	*tenees*
tennis court	teniski teren	*teneeskee teren*
terrace	terasa	*terasa*
to text	poslati SMS, tekstirati	*poslateesms, tek-steeratee*
theft	krađa	*kraja*
then	nego	*nego*
there	tamo	*tamo*
thing	stvar	*stvar*
to think	misliti	*meesleetee*
thirsty	žedno	*zhedno*
this	ovo	*ovo*
through	preko	*preko*
ticket (bus)	karta	*karta*
ticket (cinema)	karta	*karta*
ticket (parking)	karta	*karta*
ticket office	blagajna	*blagaiyna*
time	vrijeme	*vreeyeme*

time (clock)	**vrijeme**	*vreeyeme*
timetable	**raspored**	*raspored*
tip (money)	**napojnica**	***napoyneetsa***

Tip five or ten per cent in restaurants; simply round up the bill in bars and cafés.

tired	**umorno**	*oomorno*
to	**u**	*oo*
tobacco	**duhan**	*doohan*
today	**danas**	*danas*
toilet	**WC**	*ve tse*
toiletries	**toaletni predmeti**	*toaletnee predmetee*
toll	**cestarina**	*tsestareena*
tomorrow	**sutra**	*sootra*
tonight	**večeras**	*vecheras*
too	**isto**	*eesto*
tourist office	**turistički ured**	*tooreesteechkee oored*
town	**grad**	*grad*
town hall	**gradska vijećnica**	*gradska veeyechneetsa*
train	**vlak**	*vlak*
tram	**tramvaj**	*tramvaye*
to translate	**prevesti**	*prevestee*
travel	**putovanje**	*pootovanyea*
travel agency	**putnička agencija**	*pootneechka agentseeya*
true	**istinito**	*eesteeneeto*
typical	**tipično**	*teepeechno*

U

ugly	**ružno**	*roozhno*
ulcer	**čir**	*cheer*
umbrella	**kišobran**	*keeshobran*
uncomfortable	**neudobno**	*neoodobno*
unconscious	**u nesvijesti**	*u nesveeyestee*
under	**ispod**	*eespod*
underground (tube)	**podzemna željeznica**	*podzemna zhelyezneetsa*
to understand	**razumijeti**	*razoomeeyetee*
underwear	**donje rublje**	*donyea rooblyea*
unemployed	**nezaposlen/a** *m/f*	*nezaposlen/a*
unpleasant	**neugodno**	*neoogodno*
up	**gore**	*gore*
urgent	**hitno**	*heetno*
to use	**koristiti**	***koreesteetee***

When meeting, greeting and leaving, bestow a healthy handshake rather than Continental cheek kisses.

useful	**korisno**	*koreesno*
usually	**obično**	*obeechno*

V

vacant	**slobodno**	*slobodno*
vacation	**odmor**	*odmor*

vaccination	**cijepivo**	*tsiypeevo*
valid	**valjano**	*valyano*
valuables	**dragocijenosti**	*dragotseeyenostee*
value	**vrijednost**	*vreeyednost*

VAT **PDV** *pay day vay*
Fill in the right form at the point of purchase and get back some of the 22 per cent sales tax you paid, either there and then or by post and bank transfer.

vegetarian	**vegetarijanski**	*vegetareeyanskee*
vehicle	**vozilo**	*vozeelo*
very	**vrlo**	*verlo*
visa	**viza**	*veeza*
visit	**posjet**	*posyet*
to visit	**posjetiti**	*posyeteetee*
vitamin	**vitamin**	*veetameen*
to vomit	**povraćati**	*povrachatee*

W

waiter/waitress	**konobar/ica**	*konobar/eetsa*
waiting room	**čekaonica**	*chekaoneetsa*
Wales	**Vels**	*vels*
to walk	**hodati**	*hodatee*
wallet	**novčanik**	*novchaneek*
to want	**htjeti**	*htuyetee*
to wash	**prati**	*pratee*
watch	**sat**	*sat*
to watch	**gledati**	*gledatee*
water	**voda**	*voda*
water sports	**sportovi na vodi**	*sportovee na vodee*
way (manner)	**način**	*nacheen*
way (route)	**put**	*poot*
way in	**ulaz**	*oolaz*
way out	**izlaz**	*eezlaz*
weather	**vrijeme**	*vreeyeme*
web	**veb, mreža**	*veb, mrezha*
website	**internet stranica**	*eenternet straneetsa*
week	**tjedan**	*tiyedan*
weekday	**radni dan**	*radnee dan*
weekend	**vikend**	*veekend*
welcome	**dobro došli**	*dobro doshlee*
well	**dobro**	*dobro*
Welsh	**velški**	*velshkee*
west	**zapad**	*zapad*
what?	**što?**	*shto?*
wheelchair	**invalidska kolica**	*eenvaleedska koleetsa*
when?	**kada?**	*kada?*

where? **gdje?** *gdyea?*
Where did Dalmatian dogs come from? Dalmatia, of course – all 101 of them... Records show the ancient breed was here up to four thousand years ago.

which?	**koji?**	*koiyee?*

while	**dok**	*dok*
who?	**tko?**	*tko?*
why?	**zašto?**	*zashto?*
wife	**supruga**	*sooprooga*
to win	**pobijediti**	*pobeeyedeetee*
with	**s**	*s*
without	**bez**	*bez*
woman	**žena**	*zhena*
wonderful	**prekrasno**	*prekrasno*
word	**riječ**	*reeyech*
work	**rad**	*rad*
to work	**raditi**	*radeetee*
world	**svijet**	*sveeyet*
worried	**zabrinuto**	*zabreenooto*
worse	**gore**	*gore*
to write	**pisati**	*peesatee*
wrong (mistaken)	**pogrešno**	*pogreshno*

X

xenophobe	**ksenofobik**	*ksenofobeek*
xenophobia	**ksenofobija**	*ksenofobeeya*
x-ray	**rengen**	*rengen*
to x-ray	**slikati**	*sleekatee*
x-rays	**rengenske zrake**	*rengenske zrake*

Y

yacht	**jahta**	***yahta***

The yachts dock at Dubrovnik and Hvar. Steven Spielberg, Bono and the Douglases have all visited.

year	**godina**	*godeena*
yearly	**godišnje**	*godishniye*
yellow pages	**žute stranice**	*zhoote stranitse*
yes	**da**	*da*
yesterday	**jučer**	*yoocher*
yet	**još**	*yosh*
you (formal)	**Vi**	*vee*
you (informal)	**ti**	*tee*
young	**mlado**	*mlado*
your (formal)	**Vaše**	*vashe*
your (informal)	**tvoje**	*tvoyea*
youth hostel	**omladinski hostel**	*omladeenskee hostel*

Z

zebra crossing	**pješački prelaz**	***piyeshachkee prelaz***

Zebra crossings in Croatia are not inherently safe, whatever the law. Stop, look and wait.

zero	**nula**	*noola*
zip	**patentni zatvarač**	*patentnee zatvarach*
zone	**zona**	*zona*
zoo	**zoološki vrt**	*zoloshkee vert*

Croatian-English dictionary

A

alergija	*alergiya*	allergy
ali	*alee*	but
američki	*amereechkee*	American
Amerika	*amereeka*	America
apartman	*apartman*	apartment
aspirin	*aspeereen*	aspirin

Australija ***aoostraleeya*** **Australia**
More than 250,000 Croatians live Down Under, forming one of the largest expat communities.

australski	*aoostralskee*	Australian
autobus	*aootoboos*	bus
automobil	*aootomobeel*	car

B

bankomat	*bankomat*	cash point
bar	*bar*	bar (pub)
bazen	*bazen*	swimming pool
beba	*beba*	baby
benzinska postaja	*benzeenska postaya*	filling (station)
besplatno	*besplatno*	free (money)
bez	*bez*	without
bez poreza	*bez poreza*	tax free
bicikl	*beeceekl*	bicycle
bilo koji	*beelo koyee*	any
birati (broj)	*beeratee (broy)*	to dial (a number)
biti	*beetee*	to be
biti u pravu	*beetee oo pravoo*	to be right
blagajna	*blagayna*	box office, ticket office
blagovaonica	*blagovaoneetsa*	dining room
blizu	*bleezoo*	near, close by
bogato	*bogato*	rich
boja	*boya*	colour
bolesno	*bolesno*	ill
boliti	*boleetee*	to hurt
bolje	*bolye*	better
bolnica	*bolneetsa*	hospital
brat	*brat*	brother
broj	*broy*	number
brzina	*berzeena*	speed
brzo	*berzo*	fast, quick

C

carina	*tsareena*	customs
CD	*tsay day*	CD
ček	*chek*	cheque
čekaonica	*chekaoneetsa*	waiting room
centar	*tsentar*	centre
centrala	*tsentrala*	operator
cesta	*tsesta*	road

cestarina	*tsestareena*	toll
čestitam!	*chesteetam!*	congratulations!
četvrt	*chetvert*	quarter
cigara	*tseegara*	cigar
cigareta	*tseegareta*	cigarette
cijena	*tsiyena*	cost, price
čir	*cheer*	ulcer
cjepivo	*tsiyepeevo*	vaccination

D

da	*da*	yes
daleko	*daleko*	far
dama	*dama*	lady
dan	*dan*	day
danas	*danas*	today
dati	*datee*	to give
datum	*datoom*	date (calendar)
davati prednost	*davatee prednost*	to prefer
dehidrirati	*deheedreeratee*	to dehydrate
desno	*desno*	right
dezinfekcijsko sredstvo	*dezeenfektseeysko sredstvo*	disinfectant
digitron	*deegeetron*	calculator
dijete	*deeyete*	child
disko	*deesko*	disco
dizalo	*deezalo*	lift
dječak	*dyechak*	boy
dječji krevet	*dyechyee krevet*	cot
djevojčica	*dyevoycheetsa*	girl
djevojka	*dyevoyka*	girl
do	*do*	next to
dobiti	*dobeetee*	to get
dobro	*dobro*	good, well
dobro došli	*dobro doshlee*	welcome
dogovoriti	*dogovoreetee*	to arrange
dok	*dok*	while
doktor	*doktor*	doctor
dolazak	*dolazak*	arrival
dolje	*dolye*	down
donje rublje	*donye rooblye*	underwear
dosta	*dosta*	enough
drago	*drago*	kind (nice)
dragocijenosti	*dragotseeyenostee*	valuables
droga	*droga*	drug
drugo	*droogo*	other, another
država	*drzhava*	country
duhan	*doohan*	tobacco
duplo	*dooplo*	double

E

ekspresni vlak	*ekspresnee vlak*	express (train)
e-mail	*ee-mail*	e-mail
Engleska	*engleska*	England
engleski	*engleskee*	English
etiketa	*eteeketa*	label

F

faksirati	*fakseeratee*	to fax
film	*feelm*	film (camera, cinema)
foto aparat	*foto aparat*	camera
fotografija	*fotografeeya*	photo
frazeološki rječnik	*frazeoloshkee riyech-neek*	phrase book
frizer	*freezer*	hairdresser's
funta sterlinga	*foonta sterleenga*	sterling pound

G

galerija	*galereeya*	gallery

garancija ***garantsiya*** **guarantee**
Paying for items over £1,000 by credit card further protects your purchases, especially overseas.

garaža	*garazha*	garage
gdje?	*gdyea?*	where?
gladovati	*gladovatee*	to be hungry
glavni	*glavnee*	main
gledati	*gledatee*	to look, to watch
godina	*godeena*	year
godišnje	*godishnye*	yearly
godišnjica	*godishnyeetsa*	anniversary
golf	*golf*	golf
golf igralište	*golf eegraleeshte*	golf course
gore	*gore*	up, worse
gospođa	*gospoja*	madam
gospodin	*gospodeen*	sir
gotovina	*gotoveena*	cash
gotovo	*gotovo*	ready
grad	*grad*	town, city
gradska vijećnica	*gradska veeyech-neetsa*	town hall
gripa	*greepa*	flu
grupa	*groopa*	group

H

hitna pomoć	*heetna pomoch*	A&E
hitni slučaj	*heetnee sloochaye*	emergency
hitno	*heetno*	urgent, express (delivery)
hladno	*hladno*	cold, cool
hodati	*hodatee*	to walk
homoseksualno	*homoseksooalno*	homosexual
Hrvatska	*hervatska*	Croatia
hrvatski	*hervatskee*	Croatian
htjeti	*htuyetee*	to want

I

i	*ee*	and
ići	*eechee*	to go
ili	*eelee*	or
imati	*eematee*	to have

ime	*eeme*	name
informacija	*informatsiya*	information
internet stranica	*eenternet straneetsa*	website
invalidska kolica	*eenvaleedska koleetsa*	wheelchair
Irska	*eerska*	Ireland

irski *eerskee* **Irish**
Croats revel in all things shamrock; Dubrovnik, Zagreb and Pula sport their own Irish pubs.

isključeno	*eesklyoocheno*	off (switched)
ispod	*eespod*	under
istinito	*eesteeneeto*	true
isto	*eesto*	too
iza	*eeza*	back (place)
izgubiti	*izgoobeetee*	to lose
izlaz	*eezlaz*	way out
izložba	*eezlozhba*	exhibition
između	*eezmejoo*	between
iznenada	*eeznenada*	suddenly
izvoziti	*eezvozeetee*	to export

J

jahanje *yahanye* **horse riding**
Explore the countryside on an equestrian tour. Motovun Ranch in Istria is great for both beginners and experienced riders.

jahati	*yahatee*	to ride (horse)
jahta	*yahta*	yacht
javni prijevoz	*yavnee preeyevoz*	public transport
jedan	*yedan*	a, an
jedino	*yedeeno*	only
jednom	*yednom*	once
jeftino	*yefteeno*	cheap
jer	*yer*	because
jesti	*yestee*	to eat
jezik	*yezeek*	language
još	*yosh*	yet
jučer	*yoocher*	yesterday
jug	*yoog*	south
Južna Afrika	*yoozhna afreeka*	South Africa
južnoafrički	*yoozhnoafreechkee*	South African

K

kabina	*kabeena*	fitting room
kada	*kada*	bath (tub)
kada?	*kada?*	when?

kafić/kavana *kafeech/kavana* **café**
Croatian cafés often follow the grand Viennese style, with high tea and superb cakes. Pinkies out!

kako?	*kako?*	how?
kalkulator	*kalkoolator*	calculator
kapa za tuširanje	*kapa za toosheer-anyea*	bathing cap
karta	*karta*	map (road), ticket (bus, cinema, parking)
kasino	*kaseeno*	casino
kasniti	*kasneetee*	to run late
kasno	*kasno*	late (time)
katedrala	*katedrala*	cathedral
kavana	*kavana*	café
kćer	*kcher*	daughter
kemijska čistionica	*kemeeyska cheesteeoneetsa*	dry-cleaner's
kemijsko čišćenje	*kemeeysko tseeshchenye*	to dry clean
kino	*keeno*	cinema
kiosk	*keeosk*	kiosk
kiša	*keesha*	rain
kisik	*keeseek*	oxygen
kišobran	*keeshobran*	umbrella
klavijatura	*klaveeyatoora*	keyboard
klinac/klinka	*kleenats/kleenka*	kid
ključ	*klyooch*	key
klub	*kloob*	club
knjiga	*knyeega*	book
knjižnica	*knyeezhneetsa*	library
kod	*kod*	at (place)
kofer	*kofer*	suitcase
koji?	*koiyee?*	which?
kola hitne pomoći	*kola heetne pomochee*	ambulance
koliko daleko?	*koleeko daleko?*	how far?
koliko dugo?	*koleeko doogo?*	how long?
koliko veliko?	*koleeko veleeko?*	how big?
koliko?	*koleeko?*	how much?
kolovoz	*kolovoz*	August

komarac **_komarats_** **mosquito**
Croatian mosquitoes can be quite insatiable. Pack repellent sticks, citronella candles, and slow-release, electric-plug aerators.

konobar/ica	*konobar/eetsa*	waiter/waitress
kontaktirati	*kontakteeratee*	to contact
konzulat	*konzoolat*	consulate
korida	*koreeda*	bullfight
korisno	*koreesno*	useful
koristiti	*koreesteetee*	to use
kosa	*kosa*	hair
koštati	*kostatee*	to cost
krađa	*kraja*	theft
kratko	*kratko*	short
kreditna kartica	*kredeetna karteetsa*	credit card

kriminal	*kreemeenal*	crime
ksenofobija	*ksenofobeeya*	xenophobia
ksenofobik	*ksenofobeek*	xenophobe
kucati	*kootsatee*	to knock
kupaonica	*koopaonitsa*	bath (room)
kupiti	*koopeetee*	to buy
kupovina	*koopoveena*	shopping
kurs	*koors*	exchange rate
kvaliteta	*kvaleeteta*	quality
kvantiteta	*kvanteeteta*	quantity
kviz	*kveez*	quiz

L

let	*let*	flight

lijepo	*leeyepo*	nice (things), pretty

"Sunny Hvar" – an Adriatic island – boasts up to 2,715 hours of clear weather annually.

lipanj	*leepanye*	June
listopad	*leestopad*	October
ljubazno	*lyoobazno*	nice (people)
ljubiti	*lyoobeetee*	to kiss
ljudi	*lyoodee*	people
lokalno	*lokalno*	local

M

majka	*mayka*	mother
malo	*malo*	a bit, a little, little, small
manje	*manyea*	less
marka	*marka*	stamp, label
međunarodno	*mejoonarodno*	international
meduza	*medooza*	jellyfish
mehaničar	*mehaneechar*	mechanic
mekano	*mekano*	soft
menadžer	*menajer*	manager
minimum	*meeneemoom*	minimum
minuta	*meenoota*	minute
misliti	*meesleetee*	to think
mjenjačnica	*myenyachnitsa*	bureau de change
mjesto	*miyesto*	place
mjuzikl	*myoozeekl*	musical
mlado	*mlado*	young
mnogo	*mnogo*	many
mobilni telefon	*mobeelnee telefon*	mobile phone
moći	*mochee*	can (to be able)
moguće	*mogooche*	possible
moj	*moy*	my
morati	*moratee*	must
more	*more*	sea
možda	*mozhda*	maybe, perhaps
mreža	*mrezha*	web
muškarac	*mooshkarats*	man

muški WC	*mooshkee ve tse*	gents

Always carry spare change, as public conveniences may require a few coins for entry.

muzej	*moozey*	museum

N

na	*na*	on
na otvorenom	*na otvorenom*	outdoor
način	*nacheen*	way (manner)
nacionalnost	*natseeonalnost*	nationality
naj	*naye*	most
najbolje	*nayebolye*	best
naočale	*naochale*	glasses
naplata	*naplata*	charge
naplatiti	*naplateetee*	to charge
napojnica	*napoyneetsa*	tip (money)
napraviti	*napraveetee*	to make
naručiti	*naroocheetee*	to order
nazvati	*nazvatee*	to ring (phone)
nedostajati	*nedostayatee*	to miss (a person)
nego	*nego*	then
nekoliko	*nekoleeko*	some
neophodno	*neophodno*	necessary
nestalo	*nestalo*	missing
nešto	*neshto*	something
neudobno	*neoodobno*	uncomfortable, unpleasant
nezaposlen/a *m/f*	*nezaposlen/a*	unemployed
nezgoda	*nezgoda*	accident
nigdje	*neegdye*	nowhere
nikad	*neekad*	never
ništa	*neeshta*	nothing
noć	*noch*	night
noćni klub	*nochnee kloob*	nightclub
nogomet	*nogomet*	football
novac	*novats*	money
novčanica	*novchaneetsa*	note (money)
novčanik	*novchaneek*	wallet
novine	*noveene*	newspaper
novo	*novo*	new
nudistička plaža	*noodeesteechka plazha*	nudist beach

Croatia pioneered naturist tourism. Now "FKK" ("Freikörperkultur", German for 'Free Body Culture') marks over 20 official resorts and even more beaches.

nula	*noola*	zero

O

o	*o*	about (concerning)
obala	*obala*	coast

Adriatic currents flow up the Italian coast and down the Croatian, which enjoys warmer water and more fish.

obično	*obeechno*	usually
objekt	*obyekt*	object
obrazac	*obrazats*	form (document)
od	*od*	from, since
odbiti	*odbeetee*	to refuse
odgovoriti	*odgovoreetee*	to answer
odjeća	*odyecha*	clothes
odmor	*odmor*	holiday
odsutno	*odsootno*	away
odvjetnik	*odvyetneek*	lawyer
ok	*okay*	OK
oko	*oko*	around
omiljeno	*omeelyeno*	favourite
omladinski hostel	*omladeenskee hostel*	youth hostel
onesposobiti	*onesposobeetee*	disable
opljačkati	*oplyachkatee*	to rob
optičar	*opteechar*	optician's
opustiti (se)	*opoosteetee (se)*	to relax
osiguranje	*osigooranje*	insurance
osoba	*osoba*	person
osoblje	*osoblye*	staff
osobna iskaznica	*osobna eeskazneetsa*	identity card
ostaviti, otići	*ostaveetee, oteechee*	to leave
otac	*otats*	father
otišlo	*oteeshlo*	left
otkazati	*otkazatee*	to cancel

otok *otok* **island**
The Croatian coast has over 1,000 islands, some with wide-ranging services and others completely uninhabited.

otvoreno	*otvoreno*	open
otvoriti	*otvoreetee*	to open
ovdje	*ovdyea*	here
ovo	*ovo*	this
ožujak	*ozhooyak*	March

P

pab	*pab*	pub
par	*par*	pair
park	*park*	park
parkiralište	*parkeeraleeshte*	parking
parkirati	*parkeeratee*	to park
patentni zatvarač	*patentnee zatvarach*	zip
PDV	*pe de ve*	VAT
peron	*peron*	platform
pisati	*peesatee*	to write
pismo	*peesmo*	letter
pitanje	*peetanye*	question
pitati	*peetatee*	to ask
pješački prelaz	*piyeshachkee prelaz*	zebra crossing
plan grada	*plan grada*	map (city)
plan puta	*plan poota*	itinerary
platiti	*plateetee*	to pay
plaža	*plazha*	beach

plin	*pleen*	gas
plivati	*pleevatee*	to swim

pobijediti *pobeeyedeetee* **to win**

In 2005, the Croatian tennis team won its first ever Davis Cup by beating Slovakia in the final.

podne	*podne*	midday
područje	*podroochye*	area
podzemna željeznica	*podzemna zhe-lyezneetsa*	underground (tube)
pogodnosti	*pogodnostee*	facilities
pogreška	*pogreshka*	error
pogrešno	*pogreshno*	wrong (mistaken)
pojas	*poyas*	seat belt
pokazati	*pokazatee*	to show
pokraj	*pokraye*	next to, by (beside)
pokvareno	*pokvareno*	out of order, off (food)
pola	*pola*	half
polagano	*polagano*	slow
policija	*poleetseeya*	police
poljubac	*polyoobats*	kiss
pomoći	*pomochee*	to help
ponoć	*ponoch*	midnight
ponovo	*ponovo*	again
popust	*popoost*	discount, reduction
porez	*porez*	tax, duty
port	*port*	port (drink)
poruka	*porooka*	message
posao	*posao*	business
posjekotina	*posyekoteena*	cut
posjet	*posyet*	visit
posjetiti	*posyeteetee*	to visit
poslati	*poslatee*	to send
poslati SMS	*poslatee sms*	to text (send SMS)
posljednje	*poslyednyea*	last
poslovni razred	*poslovnee razred*	business class
poslužiti	*posloozheetee*	to serve
pošta	*poshta*	mail, post (office)
potpis	*potpees*	signature
potpisati	*potpeesatee*	to sign
potvrda	*potvrda*	confirmation
potvrditi	*potvrdeetee*	to confirm
povraćati	*povrachatee*	to vomit
pozivni broj	*pozeevnee broy*	area code
poznavati	*poznavatee*	to know (person)
požuri!	*pozhooree*	hurry up!
pozvoniti	*pozvoneetee*	to ring (bell)

praonica veša *praoneetsa vesha* **launderette**

Public launderettes are practically non-existent, so you must rely on your hosts or your hands.

prati	*pratee*	to wash
praznici	*prazneetsee*	holidays

predstava	*predstava*	show
preko	*preko*	through, by (via)
preko noći	*preko nochee*	overnight
preko puta	*preko poota*	opposite (place)
prekrasno	*prekrasno*	wonderful
preporučiti	*preporoocheetee*	to recommend
prevesti	*prevestee*	to translate
prezime	*prezeeme*	surname
prijatelj	*preeyatelye*	friend
prijaviti	*preeyaveetee*	to check in
prijazno	*preeyasno*	kind (nice)
prije	*preeye*	ago
prilično	*preeleechno*	quite
primiti	*preemeetee*	to receive
priroda	*preeroda*	countryside
pristanište (luka)	*preestaneeshte (looka)*	port (sea)
privatno	*preevatno*	private
privjesak za ključeve	*preevyesak za kly-oocheve*	key ring
prljavo	*prlyavo*	dirty
problem	*problem*	problem
prodati	*prodatee*	to sell
prodavaonica	*prodavaoneetsa*	shop
promijeniti	*promeeyeneetee*	to change
propustiti	*propoosteetee*	to miss (a train)

prosinac *proseenats* **December**
Snow chains are not only useful, but also necessary and required by law in winter.

prosto	*prosto*	rude
prsluk za spašavanje	*perslook za spasha-vanyea*	life jacket
prtljaga	*pertlyaga*	baggage, luggage
prva pomoć	*prva pomoch*	first aid
puno	*poono*	much

pušiti *poosheetee* **to smoke**
Croatians enjoy their cigarettes, although 70 per cent of seats in bars and restaurants must be non-smoking.

put	*poot*	way (route)
putnička agencija	*pootneechka agentseeya*	travel agency
putovanje	*pootovanyea*	journey, travel
putovnica	*pootovneetsa*	passport

R

račun	*rachoon*	bill, receipt
rad	*rad*	work
radio	*radeeo*	radio
raditi	*radeetee*	to work
radni dan	*radnee dan*	weekday
rano	*rano*	early

raskrižje	*razkreezhye*	junction
raspored	*raspored*	timetable
ravno	*ravno*	straight
razumijeti	*razoomeeyetee*	to understand
razumno	*razoomno*	sensible
recepcija	*retseptsiya*	reception
recepcionar	*retseptseeonar*	receptionist

recept *retsept* **prescription**
In Croatian, the word for prescription and recipe is the same.

red	*red*	queue
rengen	*rengen*	x-ray
rengenske zrake	*rengenske zrake*	x-rays
rezati	*rezatee*	to cut
rezervacija	*rezervatseeya*	booking, reservation
rezervirati	*rezerveeratee*	to book, to reserve
riječ	*reeyech*	word
roditelji	*rodeetelye*	parents
rujan	*rooyan*	September
ruševine	*roosheveene*	ruins
ružno	*roozhno*	ugly

S

s	*s*	with
sad	*sad*	now
samo	*samo*	only, just
samoposluga	*samoposlooga*	self-service
sastanak	*sastanak*	meeting; appointment
sat	*sat*	watch
sauna	*saoona*	sauna
sedativ	*sedateev*	sedative
sestra	*sestra*	sister
SIDA	*seeda*	AIDS
sigurno	*seegoorno*	safe
siječanj	*seeyechanye*	January
silovanje	*seelovanye*	rape
simptom	*seemptom*	symptom
sin	*seen*	son
sjedalo	*siyedalo*	seat
sjever	*syever*	north
skijanje	*skeeyanyea*	ski
Škotska	*shkotska*	Scotland
škotski	*shkotskee*	Scottish
slikati	*sleekatee*	to x-ray
sljedeće	*slyedeche*	next
slobodno	*slobodno*	available, vacant, free
slušati	*slooshatee*	to listen to
smetati	*smetatee*	to disturb
smjer puta	*smyer poota*	route
smjesta	*smyesta*	immediately
smještaj	*smyeshtiye*	accommodation
soba	*soba*	room
šoping centar	*shoping tsentar*	shopping centre
spasilac	*spaseelats*	lifeguard

spavati	*spavatee*	to sleep
spelovati	*spelovatee*	to spell

sport ***sport*** **sport**
Croats love doing and talking about sport. Tennis, skiing, basketball and football are favourites.

sportovi na vodi	*sportovee na vodee*	water sports
srpanj	*serpanye*	July
stadion	*stadeeon*	stadium
stanarina	*stanareena*	rent
stanica	*staneetsa*	station
stati	*statee*	to stop
staviti	*staveetee*	to put
šteka	*shteka*	carton (cigarettes)
šteta	*shteta*	damage
što?	*shto?*	what?
stol	*stol*	table
stranka	*stranka*	customer
stres	*stres*	stress

struja ***strooya*** **electricity**
Croatian Nikola Tesla lit up the world with his discovery of Alternating Current Electricity (EC).

studeni	*stoodenee*	November
stvar	*stvar*	thing
stvarno	*stvarno*	real
sudar	*soodar*	accident (car)
sunčane naočale	*soonchane naochale*	sunglasses
sunce	*soontse*	sun
suprug	*sooproog*	husband
supruga	*sooprooga*	wife
susresti	*soosrestee*	to meet
sutra	*sootra*	tomorrow
sve	*sve*	all
svibanj	*sveebanye*	May
sviđati se	*sveejatee se*	to like
svijet	*sveeyet*	world

T

tableta protiv bolova	*tableta proteev bolova*	painkiller
tableta za spavanje	*tableta za spavanyea*	sleeping pill
tamo	*tamo*	there
tamponi	*tamponee*	tampons

taxi ***taksee*** **taxi**
Skip the nasty surprise: ask your taxi driver for a fare estimate (cijena – ***tsiyena*****) before the journey starts.**

taxi stajalište	*taksee staiyaleeshte*	taxi rank
tekstirati	*teksteeratee*	to text
telefon	*telefon*	telephone

telefonirati	*telefoneeratee*	to phone
telefonska govornica	*telefonska govorneetsa*	telephone box
televizija	*televeezeeya*	television
tenis	*tenees*	tennis
teniski teren	*teneeskee teren*	tennis court
terasa	*terasa*	terrace
teško	*teshko*	difficult
ti	*tee*	you (informal)
tiho	*teeho*	quiet
tijekom	*teeyekom*	during
tipično	*teepeechno*	typical
tjedan	*tiyedan*	week
tko?	*tko?*	who?
toaletni predmeti	*toaletnee predmetee*	toiletries
točno	*tochno*	exactly

tramvaj ***tramvaye*** **tram**
Buses pick up where trams don't trundle. The 106 connects Kaptol to Zagreb's elegiac Mirogoj cemetery.

travanj	*travanye*	April
trčati	*terchatee*	to run
trebati	*trebatee*	to need
trenutak	*trenootak*	moment
trovanje hranom	*trovanye hranom*	food poisoning
trudna	*troodna*	pregnant
tržnica	*terzhneetsa*	market
turistički ured	*tooreesteechkee oored*	tourist office
tvoje	*tvoyea*	your (informal)

U

u	*oo*	in, to, at (time)
u nesvijesti	*u nesveeyestee*	unconscious
u redu	*oo redoo*	all right
ubod	*oobod*	(insect) bite
ubiti	*oobeetee*	to kill
učitelj	*oocheetel*	teacher
udaljen	*oodalyen*	remote
ugodno	*oogodno*	nice (people)
ugriz	*oogreez*	(dog) bite
uho	*ooho*	ear
ukrcajna karta	*ookrtsayena karta*	boarding card
ulaz	*oolaz*	way in
ulica	*oolitsa*	street
umirovljen/a	*oomeerovlyen/a*	retired
umjetnik/umjetnica	*oomyetneek/oomyet-neetsa*	artist
umjetnost	*oomyetnost*	art
umorno	*oomorno*	tired
unajmiti	*oonayemeetee*	to hire, to rent
unutra	*oonootra*	inside
upaliti auto	*oopaleetee aooto*	to start (car)

upit	*oopeet*	query
upomoć!	*oopomoch!*	help!
upute	*oopoote*	directions
uraditi	*ooradeetee*	to do
ured	*oored*	office
ured za izgubljeno-nađeno	*oored za eez-gooblyeno-najeno*	lost and found property (office)
uskoro	*ooskoro*	soon
usluga	*ooslooga*	service
usne	*oosne*	lips
usta	*oosta*	mouth
uvesti	*oovestee*	to import
uvijek	*ooveejek*	always
uzbuna	*oozboona*	alarm
uzeti	*oozetee*	to take
uzrast	*oozrast*	age (person)
uživati	*oozheevatee*	to enjoy

V

val	*val*	wave
valjano	*valyano*	valid
valuta	*valoota*	currency
vani	*vanee*	outside
Vaše	*vashe*	your (formal)
vatra	*vatra*	fire
važno	*vazhno*	important
veb	*veb*	web
večera	*vechera*	dinner
večeras	*vecheras*	tonight
vegetarijanski	*vegetareeyanskee*	vegetarian
veleposlanstvo	*veleposlanstvo*	embassy
veliko	*veleeko*	big

veljača — ***velyacha*** — **February**
Croatia celebrates carnival month with enthusiasm. Samobor holds one of the best-known festivities.

Vels	*vels*	Wales
velški	*velshkee*	Welsh
vena	*vena*	vein
veselo	*veselo*	jolly
veslanje	*veslanye*	rowing
Vi	*vee*	you (formal)
vidimo se	*veedeemo se*	see you later
vijesti	*veeyestee*	news
vikend	*veekend*	weekend
vinograd	*veenograd*	vineyard
više	*veeshe*	more
visoko	*veesoko*	high, tall
vitamin	*veetameen*	vitamin
viza	*veeza*	visa

vjenčano *v<u>ye</u>nchano* married

Croatian destination-weddings are becoming more popular. The British Embassy website offers some advice (www.britishembassy.gov.uk/croatia).

vjerojatno	*viy<u>e</u>royatno*	probably
vjetar	*v<u>ye</u>tar*	wind
vlak	*vlak*	train
vlasnik	*vl<u>a</u>sneek*	owner
voće	*v<u>o</u>che*	fruit
voda	*v<u>o</u>da*	water
vodeni skuter	*v<u>o</u>deni sk<u>oo</u>ter*	jet ski
vodenica	*vod<u>e</u>neetsa*	water mill
vodič	*v<u>o</u>deech*	guide
vodopad	*v<u>o</u>dopad*	waterfall
vozač	*v<u>o</u>zach*	driver
vozačka dozvola	*v<u>o</u>zachka d<u>o</u>zvola*	driving licence
vozilo	*v<u>o</u>zeelo*	vehicle
voziti	*v<u>o</u>zeetee*	to drive, to ride (scooter)
vožnja biciklom	*v<u>o</u>zhnya beets<u>ee</u>klom*	cycling
vratiti (novac)	*vr<u>a</u>teetee (n<u>o</u>vats)*	to refund
vreća za spavanje	*vr<u>e</u>cha za sp<u>a</u>vanye*	sleeping bag
vrh	*vrh*	summit
vrhnje	*<u>v</u>rhnye*	cream
vrijednost	*vr<u>ee</u>yednost*	value
vrijeme	*vreey<u>e</u>me*	time, weather
vrlo	*v<u>er</u>lo*	very, most
vrsta	*v<u>er</u>sta*	kind (sort)
vruće	*vr<u>oo</u>che*	hot
vrućina	*vroochee<u>ee</u>na*	heat
vuna	*v<u>oo</u>na*	wool

W

WC	*ve tse*	toilet

Z

za	*za*	for
zabava	*z<u>a</u>bava*	party
zabavan	*z<u>a</u>bavan*	fun
zabaviti	*z<u>a</u>baveetee*	to entertain
zaboravit	*zab<u>oo</u>raveet*	forget
zabrinuto	*z<u>a</u>breenooto*	worried
zadnji/posljednji	*z<u>a</u>dnyee/poslyednyee*	the last
zahvala	*z<u>a</u>hvala*	thanks
zakašnjelo	*zak<u>a</u>shnyelo*	late (delayed)
zaključati	*zakly<u>oo</u>chatee*	to lock
žalba	*zh<u>a</u>lba*	complaint

žaliti se *zh<u>a</u>leetee se* to complain

Every hotel and restaurant must by law have a Book of Complaints. Only file your grievance if it's serious – you'll be creating bureaucratic nightmare for the owner otherwise.

zamijenit	*zameeyeneet*	change (money)

zanimljivo ***zaneemlyeevo*** **interesting**
Inventive Croatians include the creators of the screw propeller, mechanical pencil and the first working parachute.

zapad	*zapad*	west
zapaliti	*zapaleetee*	to burn
započeti	*zapochetee*	to start
zarazno	*zarazno*	contagious
zašto?	*zashto?*	why?
zatražiti	*zatrazheetee*	to request
zatvoreno	*zatvoreno*	closed, shut
zatvoriti	*zatvoreetee*	to close
zaustaviti	*zaoostaveetee*	to stop (someone)
završiti	*zaversheetee*	to finish
žedno	*zhedno*	thirsty
željeznica	*zhelyezneetsa*	railway
žena	*zhena*	woman
ženski wc	*zhenskee ve tse*	ladies (toilets)
zidine	*zeedeene*	walls
žilet	*zheelet*	razor blade
zima	*zeema*	winter
zimovanje	*zeemovanye*	winter holiday
životinje	*zheevoteenye*	animals
znak	*znak*	sign

znati ***znatee*** **to know**
Get to know Zagreb's art scene with music, film and underground beats at one of the city's cult clubs.

zona	*zona*	zone
zoološki vrt	*zoloshkee vert*	zoo
zora	*zora*	dawn

zračna luka ***zrachna looka*** **airport**
Rijeka airport is on Krk, Croatia's largest and northernmost island, which is connected to the mainland by bridge.

zračna pošta	*zrachna poshta*	airmail
zrakoplov	*zrakoplov*	aeroplane
žute stranice	*zhoote straneetse*	yellow pages
zvati	*zvatee*	to call

Quick reference

Numbers

0	Nula	*noola*
1	Jedan	*yedan*
2	Dva	*dva*
3	Tri	*tree*
4	Četiri	*cheteeree*
5	Pet	*pet*
6	Šest	*shest*
7	Sedam	*sedam*
8	Osam	*osam*
9	Devet	*devet*
10	Deset	*deset*
11	Jedanaest	*yedanaest*
12	Dvanaest	*dvanaest*
13	Trinaest	*treenaest*
14	Četrnaest	*cheternaest*
15	Petnaest	*petnaest*
16	Šesnaest	*shesnaest*
17	Sedamnaest	*sedamnaest*
18	Osamnaest	*osamnaest*
19	Devetnaest	*devetnaest*
20	Dvadeset	*dvadeset*
21	Dvadeset i jedan	*dvadeset ee yedan*
30	Trideset	*treedeset*
40	Četrdeset	*cheterdeset*
50	Pedeset	*pedeset*
60	Šezdeset	*shezdeset*
70	Sedamdeset	*sedamdeset*
80	Osamdeset	*osamdeset*
90	Devedeset	*devedeset*
100	Sto	*sto*
1000	Tisuću	*teesoochoo*

1st	Prvi	*pervee*
2nd	Drugi	*droogee*
3rd	Treći	*trechee*
4th	Četvrti	*chetvertee*
5th	Peti	*petee*

Weights & measures

gram (=0.03oz)	**gram**	*gram*
kilogram (=2.2lb)	**kilogram**	*keelogram*
dekagram (=0.022lb)	**dekagram**	*dekagram*
centimetre (=0.4in)	**centimetar**	*tsenteemetar*
metre (=1.1yd)	**metar**	*metar*
kilometre (=0.6m)	**kilometar**	*keelometar*
litre (=2.1pt)	**litra**	*leetra*

Days & time

Monday	**Ponedjeljak**	*ponediyelyak*
Tuesday	**Utorak**	*ootorak*
Wednesday	**Srijeda**	*sreeyeda*
Thursday	**Četvrtak**	*chetvertak*
Friday	**Petak**	*petak*
Saturday	**Subota**	*soobota*
Sunday	**Nedjelja**	*nediyelya*

What time is it?	**Koliko je sati?**	*koleeko ye satee?*
(Four) o'clock	**(Četiri) sata**	*(cheteeree) sata*
Quarter past/to (six)	**(Šest) i petnaest**	*(shest) ee petnaest*
Half past (eight)	**(Osam) i trideset**	*(osam) ee treedeset*
Quarter to (ten)	**(Devet) i četrdeset pet**	*(devet) ee cheterdeset pet*

morning	**jutro**	*yootro*
afternoon	**poslijepodne**	*posleeyepodne*
evening	**večer**	*vecher*
night	**noć**	*noch*

Clothes size conversions

Women's clothes	34	36	38	40	42	44	46	48
equiv. UK size	6	8	10	12	14	16	18	20
Men's jackets	44	46	48	50	52	54	56	58
equiv. UK size	34	36	38	40	42	44	46	48
Men's shirts	36	37	38	39	40	41	42	43
equiv. UK size	14	14.5	15	15.5	16	16.5	17	17.5
Shoes	37	38	39	40	41/42	43	44	45
equiv. UK size	4	5	6	7	8	9	10	11